W9-DBE-064

The Land and People of
TURKEY

PORTRAITS OF THE NATIONS

The Land and People of®

TURKEY

by *William Spencer*

J. B. LIPPINCOTT   NEW YORK

Country maps by Robert Romagnoli.
Photo research by Rod Beebe.

Every effort has been made to locate the copyright holders of all copyrighted materials and to secure the necessary permission to reproduce them. In the event of any questions arising as to their use, the publisher will be glad to make necessary changes in future printings and editions.

Map on page 69 is adapted from *Armenia: Crossroads of Cultures*, by Anahid V. Ordjanian, and used by permission of Eleanora Ordjanian. Quote on page 99 is from *Human Landscapes*, copyright © 1982 by Randy Blasing and Mutlu Konuk. Reprinted by permission of Persea Books, Inc. Quote at top of page 168 is from *Istanbul Boy*, published by and used with the permission of The Center for Middle Eastern Studies at the University of Texas at Austin. Quote on page 48 is taken from *Tamar and Other Poems*, by Robinson Jeffers. Copyright © by Peter G. Boyle.

THE LAND AND PEOPLE OF
is a registered trademark of
Harper & Row, Publishers, Inc.

The Land and People of Turkey
Copyright © 1990 by William Spencer
All rights reserved.
Printed in the United States of America.
For information address J. B. Lippincott Junior Books,
10 East 53rd Street, New York, N.Y. 10022.
10 9 8 7 6 5 4 3 2 1
First Edition

Library of Congress Cataloging-in-Publication Data
Spencer, William, 1922–
    The land and people of Turkey / by William Spencer.
        p.   cm. — (Portraits of the nations series)
    Summary: Introduces the history, geography, people, culture, government, and economy of Turkey.
    Bibliography: p.
    ISBN 0-397-32363-8 : $ — ISBN 0-397-32364-6 (lib. bdg.) : $
    1. Turkey—Juvenile literature.   [1. Turkey.]   I. Title.
II. Series.
DR417.S67 1990   89-2421
956.1—dc19   CIP
                                                AC

TO MY WIFE
Elizabeth

We have climbed together
Up the steep cobblestones of Besiktas
Sailed smooth seas to Byzantium
Journeys of joy without number
And always your presence
Enriches my days

Acknowledgments

The Turkish proverb "a good companion shortens the longest road" aptly describes the help I have received from many hands in writing this book. My thanks go especially to Warren and Barbara Walker, Director and Curator respectively of the Archive of Turkish Oral Narrative at Texas Tech University for their invaluable assistance with sources and reference materials and their vast store of personal experiences in Turkey. Paul Magnarella, of the University of Florida, helped clarify points on the Turkish language from which my text has benefitted. Erol Sahinoglu of Winter Park, Florida, guided me through the intricacies of the carpet craft/industry. Lorrin and Doris Riggs generously loaned me the family record "Shepard of Aintab", which recounts the important services of one of the first American medical missionaries to the Ottoman Empire; my thanks go to them for this valuable guide into the recent Turkish past. Special thanks also to Marc Aronson, my editor at Harper & Row, for breathing life and order into a disjointed earlier version of this portrait. Lastly my debt to my wife Elizabeth is beyond measure. Her fine sense of style, accuracy of thought, clarity of phrase and grace under pressure are apparent on every page. This book is hers as well as mine, and I salute her with a well-deserved *çok teşekkür ederim!*

Contents

THE WORLD

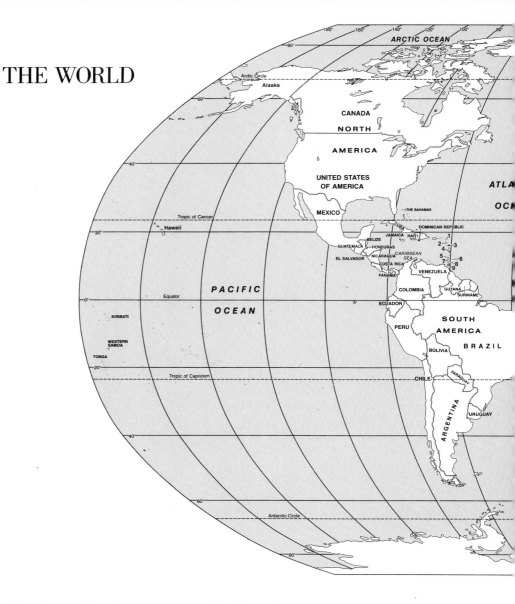

This world map is based on a projection developed by Arthur H. Robinson. The shape of each country and its size, relative to other countries, are more accurately expressed here than in previous maps. The map also gives equal importance to all of the continents, instead of placing North America at the center of the world. *Used by permission of the Foreign Policy Association.*

Legend

——— International boundaries

---------- Disputed or undefined boundaries

Projection: Robinson

0   1000   2000   3000 Miles

0   1000   2000   3000 Kilometers

Caribbean Nations

1. Anguilla
2. St. Christopher and Nevis
3. Antigua and Barbuda
4. Dominica
5. St. Lucia
6. Barbados
7. St. Vincent
8. Grenada
9. Trinidad and Tobago

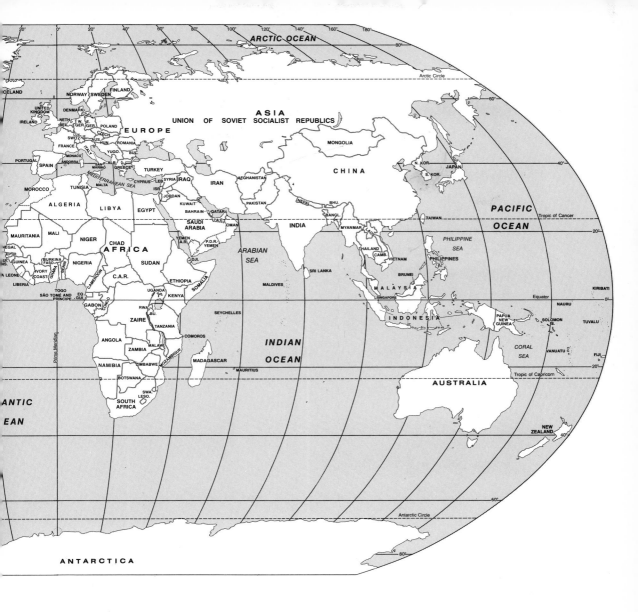

Abbreviations

ALB. —Albania
AUS. —Austria
BANGL.—Bangladesh
BEL. —Belgium
BHU. —Bhutan
BU. —Burundi
BUL. —Bulgaria
CAMB.—Cambodia

C.A.R. —Central African Republic
CZECH. —Czechoslovakia
DJI. —Djibouti
E.GER. —East Germany
EQ. GUI.—Equatorial Guinea
GUI. BIS.—Guinea Bissau
HUN. —Hungary
ISR. —Israel

LEB. —Lebanon
LESO. —Lesotho
LIE. —Liechtenstein
LUX. —Luxemburg
NETH. —Netherlands
N. KOR. —North Korea
P.D.R.–YEMEN—People's Democratic Republic of Yemen

RWA. —Rwanda
S. KOR. —South Korea
SWA. —Swaziland
SWITZ. —Switzerland
U.A.E. —United Arab Emirates
W. GER. —West Germany
YEMEN A.R.—Yemen Arab Republic
YUGO. —Yugoslavia

Mini Facts

OFFICIAL NAME: Republic of Turkey *(Türkiye Cumhuriyeti)*

LOCATION: Extreme southeastern Europe and southwestern Asia (Anatolian Peninsula). The two parts of the country are separated by the Straits (Dardanelles), the Sea of Marmara, and the Bosporus. Land borders are with Bulgaria and Greece on the west, the Soviet Union, Iran, and Iraq on the east, and Syria to the southeast.

AREA: 301,380 square miles (780,576 square kilometers)

CAPITAL: Ankara (population of Greater Ankara, 3,462,000, 1985 census)

POPULATION: 55,377,000 (1985 census)

POPULATION GROWTH RATE: 2.4 percent annually

MAJOR LANGUAGE: Turkish

RELIGION: 99 percent Islamic; small Jewish and Christian minorities

TYPE OF GOVERNMENT: Republic, founded 1923

HEAD OF STATE: President (seven-year term)

HEAD OF GOVERNMENT: Prime Minister (five-year term)

LEGISLATURE: Legislative power vested in the Grand National Assembly, which has 50 members elected for five-year terms.

POLITICAL PARTIES: Motherland (majority party), True Path, Social Democratic Party

PER CAPITA INCOME: $1,300 annually

LITERACY RATE: 70 percent urban, 50 percent rural

MONETARY UNIT: lira (TL), divided into 100 kuruş; exchange rate (1989), TL 2,059 = U.S. $1.00

EXPORTS: $8 billion (1988)

IMPORTS: $11 billion (1988)

Preface

Thirty-five years ago we had just arrived in Ankara, Turkey's capital, on the English-language teaching assignment that led to publication of an earlier book in this series. Housing was in short supply in the city, just beginning its rapid growth as new arrivals crowded in from the countryside. The artificially high exchange rate of 2.80 Turkish liras to $1.00 put an unexpected crimp in our budget; we needed not only acceptable accommodations but also inexpensive ones. Day after day we tramped the streets following up leads or notices that proved fruitless. We had just about given up when we spotted a sign in the upstairs picture window of a brand-new building at the far end of an unpaved lane: "To Let," it read, *Güzel Manzara*—Beautiful View." We hurried down the lane, found the prospective landlord—fortunately he knew a few words of English—and asked to rent the place on the spot. For once luck was on our side; we were first in line, and the price was right.

Güzel Manzara was our first window into Turkey and the Turks. The view was beautiful indeed, with the brown-and-green plain of Ankara unrolling like a carpet all the way to distant mountains, sheep and goats feeding in nearby fields, and on clear days the silvery glint of water from the new dam. There were empty lots around us where our children played with their Turkish peers, teaching them *bezbol* and learning *futbol* (we would call it soccer) in return. One day a wandering trainer came down from the mountains with his dancing bear to perform for us; the bear wrestled with his master and then danced a sort of solo gavotte, as a huge crowd gathered. On another day it was a caravan of Gypsies, and on winter nights we could hear wolves howling not too far from our door.

Time passes, with its inevitable growth and change, and when we returned to Ankara in the 1970's, we could not even find our building. It had been swallowed up in a forest of new concrete construction, sprouting clotheslines, and TV antennae. The open fields were gone, the lanes paved and renamed, our bakery and one-room grocery replaced by an arcaded shopping mall. Yet in an indefinable way *Güzel Manzara* was still there, in the mind's eye. Through it we could draw up memories of Turks whose lives we had shared for a time, and also turn it like a double glass to draw a newer portrait.

Portraits of nations, like those of individuals, age between sittings. Thirty years, in our hurry-up, high-technology world, is a full measure of aging. Much has changed in Turkey in that period, for good as well as for bad. The view from the picture window today overlooks dams and highways, shopping centers and office buildings not unlike our own. Urban sprawl is in full sway in Turkey as elsewhere. But there is still that goodly view of distant mountains, and magnificent ruins all around, to remind the Turks of their past as they go about building a new democratic nation.

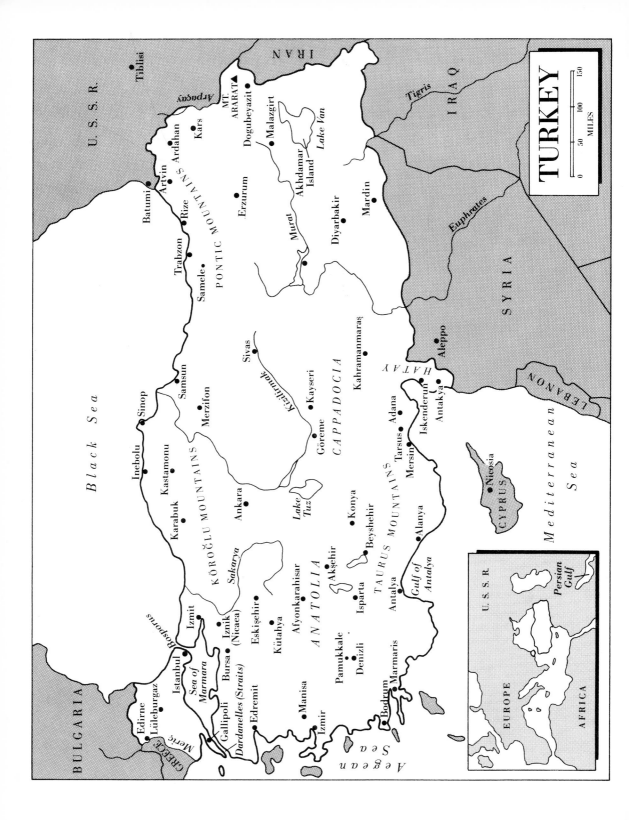

Prologue

God finds a low branch for the bird that cannot fly.

Turkish proverb

Turkey begins at Istanbul. Once the city was called Byzantium, and then Constantinople; the modern Turks settled on Istanbul, meaning literally "into the city," *the* city. There is no other city like it in the world, for it straddles two continents, at the southernmost point where Europe and Asia meet, along the narrow waterway called the Bosporus (*Boğaziçi,* "within the throat" in Turkish). Although Turkish territory extends westward from Istanbul for nearly two hundred miles into Europe, the city symbolizes the two faces of Turkey, one turned resolutely to the west, the other looking eastward into Asia.

They were going to Istanbul together. Yes, that was it! Salih on foot, the little seagull flying above him, wings outstretched. Over hill and down dale they went, until they came to Istanbul city and stopped at the foot of the Bosporus bridge. Ships were sailing under it. The sea was gilded with

Galata Bridge on the Golden Horn, Istanbul.   Maury Englander

myriad lights from the houses on the shore, the passing cars, the stars. The seagull darted in and out of the lights, vanishing into the velvety depths of the night sky. (Yashar Kemal, Seagull.*)*

Istanbul seen from close range is a startling mixture of old and new, twentieth-century technology and sixteenth-century architecture. Cars, trucks, and buses rumble across the bridges over the Bosporus, while below them huge ferryboats belching smoke zigzag along the water, carrying commuters, farm produce, packages, and even live goats or chickens to various destinations. Pedestrians stroll along the older (1912) Galata Bridge over the Golden Horn, Istanbul's inner harbor. Vendors hawk *simits*, a kind of crescent-shaped doughnut, or sell grilled

A nineteenth-century engraving shows a similar view of the city and the river.   Culver Pictures, Inc.

fish in baskets or rent tackle to would-be fishermen trying their luck in the inky waters below, while the small fish restaurants and *çayhanesi* (teahouses) on the lower levels of the bridge are jammed with customers day and night.

Above this hubbub of honking horns, hooting ferryboats, shouting vendors, and bleating goats rises the magnificent skyline of Istanbul. It is a skyline of domes and pointed spires spread along the city's seven hills. The domes are those of mosques, the Turkish houses of worship. Although Turkey forms part of the eastern frontier of Europe with Asia, it differs from other European countries in being spiritually and culturally part of the world of Islam, a monotheistic religion founded in Arabia fourteen centuries ago. The pointed spires are called minarets, from an ancient Persian word meaning lighthouse. Following strict religious requirements, a prayer caller climbs to the upper balcony of one of the minarets of each mosque five times a day to call the Turks to prayer, adding to the cacophony of the city's sounds. Dome and spire have combined to give Istanbul a stunning visual beauty that is enhanced by the red-tile roofs of venerable mansions and palaces, the glass, steel, and concrete of modern hotels and office buildings, and the deep blue line of the Bosporus far below.

Thirty years ago, despite the narrowing of the world subsequently through TV and other media, Turkey was probably a more familiar country to Americans than it is today. The Turks had fought alongside American GIs in the Korean War and had distinguished themselves for bravery under fire. But Turkish-American relations have changed considerably since that time. Not only can the friendship no longer be taken for granted, but also there have been strong disagreements between the two governments over such political issues as Cyprus. These disagreements often have come about because of different views of foreign policy and national self-interest.

Turkey is a country of great complexity and is endlessly fascinating. Why is this the case? It is in part due to its long history and geographical diversity, but more importantly it is because the country has a modern-day mixture of vigorous peoples representing many different cultures and traditions. This diversity has hampered political unification in the past, but in terms of Turkey's social and cultural heritage the intermingling of different ethnic groups has been a source of strength. Therefore in this book when Turks are referred to it is a term of *inclusion*. In the United States when one refers to Americans, it is recognized that we come from European, African, Hispanic, Asian, and Native American ancestries but are still thought of as Americans. Similarly, with the exception of a small ethnic-minority population, the

Turks—who spring from a variety of groups—have become a particular people, attached to a particular country.

Life has not been easy for the Turks in the twentieth century. They are a proud people with a proud heritage. For many centuries—until the end of the First World War—Turkey was known as the Ottoman Empire. It was a superpower in its day, controlling large parts of Europe, Asia, the Middle East, and northern Africa. The empire finally collapsed after the war, but out of its ruins was created a modern democratic republic. There are flaws in Turkey's democracy, as one might expect from a people accustomed to autocratic rule throughout most of their history. Also, the strategic location of the country at the meeting point of continents and waterways inevitably involves the Turks in world affairs. But despite these obstacles they have come a long way toward building a stable political system and a viable economy.

Nine-Tenths Asia

Among the nations of the world Turkey is large, with an area of over 300,000 square miles (780,000 square kilometers). It is somewhat larger than Texas but has three times the population. Nine tenths of Turkey is located in Asia; the remainder comprises the province *(vilayet)* of Thrace, in extreme southeastern Europe. European and Asiatic Turkey are physically separated by the Bosporus, the outlet for the Black Sea, and the Dardanelles or Straits, the eastern outlet for the Mediterranean Sea.

The Bosporus and the Straits are linked by the Sea of Marmara, the entire stretch from the Mediterranean being considered Turkish territorial waters. The Straits and the Bosporus have been coveted and fought over since ancient times. In the days before nuclear weapons and air power they were the only outlet for Russian ships based in the otherwise enclosed Black Sea. Today Soviet warships and merchant vessels are heavy users of these waterways, but the Turks can forbid passage if they

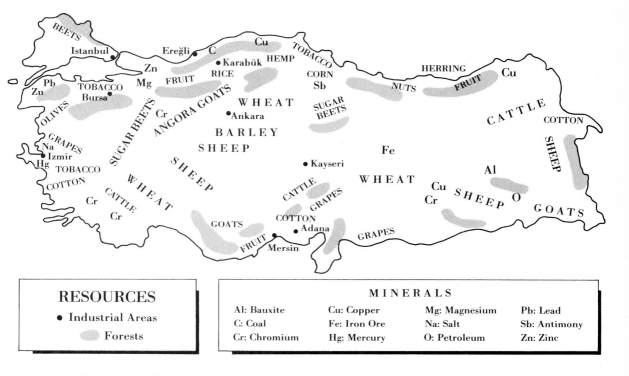

feel threatened by their powerful neighbor to the north.

Asiatic Turkey consists of a peninsula that sticks out like a large hump on the flank of Asia. (Geographers with imagination might describe it as a buffalo with a hump.) The ancient Greeks and Romans called it Asia Minor; to them it seemed like a miniature version of the vast Asian continent. Asia Minor is a plateau, averaging 3,600 feet (1,100 meters) in elevation, bounded on three sides by seas: the Black Sea on the north, the Aegean on the west, and the Mediterranean on the south side. Coastal mountain ranges wall off the plateau on its north and south sides; the only easy access inland is along the broad river valleys of the Aegean coast. With mountains, seacoasts, inland plains, and semidesert steppe all in close proximity, Asia Minor is clearly a continent in miniature.

Geographical Regions

Due to its size and diversity Turkey has a number of distinct geographical regions. The European region, Thrace *(Trakya)* is an extension of the Balkan lands of eastern Europe, rolling country well suited to growing wheat and other cereal grains. Thrace is also famous for its green melons, white fleshed like honeydews and incredibly sweet. The principal city is Edirne, formerly called Adrianople, an ancient Roman city that was the first European capital of the Ottoman Empire, predecessor of the Turkish Republic.

The Aegean coast, along with Istanbul and its hinterland, is Turkey's most densely populated and developed. Izmir (ancient Smyrna), its major city, is Turkey's major port and third largest city (1.9 million people). The Aegean region and the Çukurova Plain around Adana, in the Mediterranean region, are the principal areas of production of cotton, the country's main agricultural export crop and the basis for the growing textile industry. (Turkey ranked seventh in the world in cotton production in 1988, with 3.5 percent of total output.)

The Aegean coast is deeply indented, with long narrow peninsulas that reach out like bony fingers into the sea. Travel between them is faster by boat than by car. They were formed by the geologic cracking of the earth eons ago due to the cooling of layers of volcanic lava deposited there. The cooling process also created many small islands close to the shore. Geographically—and geologically—these islands are extensions of the Turkish mainland, but in the peace treaty between Turkey and various European powers after World War I that established the republic, the islands were awarded to Greece, on the grounds that their population was ethnically Greek. Although some of the is-

Club Med resort at Yeni Foca (New Foca), one of the fine tourist facilities on Turkey's Aegean coast. Turkish Tourism Office

Two men meeting on a road just outside of Artvin, located in northeastern Turkey near the Black Sea.   Joseph Lawton

lands, such as Samos, are within eyesight of the Turkish coast, they belong to Greece, and a passport is required for the short boat ride over from the mainland.

The Aegean coast is Turkey's longest, 1,744 miles (2,805 km.)—longer than that of California. The Black Sea coast, considerably shorter because it is relatively straight (1,053 miles; 1,695 km.) extends from the Bosporus west to the Bulgarian border and east to the Soviet border. This region is the country's rainiest, with over 100 inches (250 centimeters) of rain annually. Three important crops in Turkish agriculture,

Pamukkale, or "Cotton Castle" near Denizli in the southwestern Aegean region, is an incredible natural phenomenon: a series of calcified "springs" and "waterfalls" dropping from a 330-foot (100-meter) cliff onto the plateau and forming stalactites like organ pipes.
Turkish Tourism Office

· 10 ·

cherries, hazelnuts, and tea, are grown there, since they require a humid climate. Turkey is the major world producer of hazelnuts, with 65 percent of the market.

The hazeltree is sacred in many lands because of its purported mystic powers. The Arabs believe that it protects a person from evil. The French call it the "magic stick," claiming that anyone using it to dowse for water underground will always be successful. The Romans burned hazel boughs for good luck at weddings, and the Turks say that it was one of the fruit trees in the Garden of Eden.

Other important Black Sea crops are tobacco, tea, rice, and various fruits. Like the melons of Thrace, the peaches of Samsun and Merzifon have a well-deserved reputation. The region around Sinop is heavily planted in tobacco fields, perhaps explaining why Turks are heavy smokers, although much of the crop is exported.

Turkish coffee is not the national drink, as one might expect, because the country does not grow coffee and must import the beans from elsewhere. Coffee drinking is reserved for special occasions due to its expense. It marks the end of the hospitality ritual for guests, brewed twice after a meal and poured into tiny cups. The Turkish proverb "A cup of coffee commits one to forty years of friendship" is an apt description of the role of coffee in national life.

Tea, however, is more important than coffee in national business and social life. Turks drink tea all day long, in offices, shops, restaurants, and innumerable small *çayhanesi.* It is even delivered to office workers on small brass trays by runners called *çaycis.* The tea they drink is grown on the steep hillsides near Rize, on large plantations, picked by country women in bright-colored shawls and bloomers, brought to nearby tea processing plants and subsequently shipped to town and

Men gathered in a small square in the old section of Diyarbakir in the southeastern part of Turkey. Groups of men spending afternoons like this may be found throughout the country.   Joseph Lawton

city markets and shops. To illustrate the importance of tea to the Turks, some years ago the distribution system went awry, shipments were held up, shortages developed, and business life practically came to a stop. A greater calamity occurred in 1987, when dangerously high levels of radioactivity were discovered in Turkish tea samples after the explosion at the Chernobyl nuclear reactor in the Soviet Union, and all tea was taken off the market. One observer said it was as if millions of people simultaneously quit smoking!

The Mediterranean Region

Turkey's Mediterranean coast extends from the yachting port of Marmaris, where the Aegean and Mediterranean meet, eastward along a series of gently curving bays to the important port of Iskenderun, and from there southward to the Syrian border. The tourist industry, one of the country's major sources of revenue, describes it as "The Turquoise Coast" because of the blue-green water, white sand beaches, small coves and caves, and the nearby Taurus Mountains as backdrop. The coastal section between the old walled cities of Antalya and Alanya, linked by a scenic highway that winds through orange and lemon groves and the ruins of Greco-Roman cities, recalls the French and Italian rivieras in the western Mediterranean. But in addition to the importance of the region to tourism, it grows most of Turkey's citrus fruit, bananas, pineapples, and other tropical fruit crops.

Enclosed within the mountain walls that encircle the coastal regions is the Turkish heartland. The Turks do not refer to it as Asia Minor but as Anadolu or, in English, Anatolia. The name means "land of the rising sun." As the Turkish tribes traveled west with the sun at their backs, searching for water and pasturage for their flocks and safety from their enemies, Anatolia probably reminded them of their Central Asian homeland, with only isolated mountains, vast shimmering salt lakes, and the occasional shallow river to break the monotony of the steppe that rolled endlessly toward the horizon. Even today much of it has not changed. The plateau has been settled, fought over, plowed and devastated, replowed and cultivated, for over nine thousand years; and for earlier eons sun, wind, and rain worked over the landscape as if with hammer, chisel, and paintbrush. The result is a land that still seems vast and

The beach at Antalya on the "Turkish Riviera." Turkish Tourism Office

timeless despite the inroads of civilization and modern technology. There is an emptiness to Anatolia that brings with it a gift that is rare in our noisy world—the gift of silence.

Inland Anatolia grows the greater part of Turkey's wheat and other cereal grains and has most of its livestock. In many areas the shepherd is still king, with his huge mastifflike Anatolian sheepdog wearing a spiked iron collar to protect him from the attacks of wolves. Settlements are far apart, and the major cities—Ankara, Konya, Kayseri—although bursting at the seams with people, are still remote from each other, isolated urban areas in semidesert.

The heartland also contains the bulk of the country's mineral resources. Turkey has a near monopoly on the world's supply of boron, a rare element important in metallurgy and the hardening of steels. There are also commercially valuable deposits of bauxite (aluminum ore), chromium ore, copper, iron ore, magnesium, manganese, and such rare metals as tungsten, perlite, and cinnabar. Turkey ranks fourth in world production of chromium, which is used in the manufacture of high-technology steels and other alloys.

Crafts Specialties

Certain Anatolian subregions have been known since ancient times for unusual or specialized products. Near the city of Eskişehir, for example, are the world's largest deposits of meerschaum, a soft claylike form of magnesium silicate that is carved into pipes by skilled craftsmen. Meerschaum pipes age nut brown from their original white as they are used, and always smoke cool and sweet. A law now forbids the export of block (uncarved) meerschaum, since that would take jobs away from the artisans of Eskişehir.

Rugged countryside between Kars and Artvin, eastern Anatolia.   Turkish Tourism Office

Above: *This overview of the natural rock formations in the Cappadocia region shows the landscape in which the many caves are placed.*   Joseph Lawton

Right: *Distinctive cave dwellings in Cappadocia. The landscape of this region is spotted with hundreds of these caves.*   Joseph Lawton

Another specialized product is the pottery made in Kütahya, in west-central Anatolia. Pottery making is an ancient and honored tradition in Anatolia, dating back to the earliest settlements. The potters of Iznik (Nicaea) were famous for the blue faïence (glazed earthenware) that adorns the finest mosques and public buildings of Istanbul and other cities. But Kütahya, originally developed by Armenians, has become synonymous with Turkish pottery in the twentieth century. Kütahya plates, bowls, and serving dishes, decorated with birds, flowers, or

calligraphic designs in soft pastel greens, blues, and pale reds, are attractive and popular with visitors as well as Turks. Many of the Kütahya potters learned their trade as apprentices to their fathers, and the visitor to the potteries often finds two generations from the same family working side by side at their wheels.

The city of Afyon, in southwestern Anatolia, illustrates an interesting aspect of the close relationship between geography and agriculture. "Afyon" means "poppy" in Turkish, and in the blooming season the city is surrounded by fields of waving purple and white poppies. For centuries Afyon farmers harvested raw opium from the plants, sometimes for sale to legitimate laboratories but at other times to smugglers who carried it to eastern Asian or Arabian buyers. The poppy was the only source of income for these growers. But the enormous growth of the worldwide drug trade brought a huge demand for Turkish opium; 80 percent of the illegal opium smuggled to American markets came originally from the Afyon fields. The Turkish government, under pressure from the U.S. government, agreed to ban poppy cultivation entirely in 1972, creating bad feelings between the two countries. The ban was lifted in 1974 after other crops were tested in the area with relatively little success, due in part to the particularly poor nature of the soil and the undependable rainfall, but also to stubborn resistance from Afyon poppy growers, a situation similar to that of coca growers in Bolivia today. Today about 200,000 acres are devoted to opium production from poppies under strict Turkish government controls. The opium gum is no longer taken directly from the flower; instead, government agents buy the poppy pods, called "opium straw," from the growers and take them to factories, which then process the straw into raw opium concentrate for export to pharmaceutical companies.

Since 1974 visitors to Afyon are again able to enjoy two unexpected byproducts of the City's major "industry"—unleavened bread made from

Central Anatolia includes the Turkish capital, Ankara, its metropolitan area exploding at the seams with 3.46 million people, and various smaller cities such as Konya (350,000 people) and Kayseri (300,000 people). These figures underline not only the high birth rate but also the changing nature of Turkish society as rural people migrate to the cities.

Eastern and southeastern Anatolia are worlds apart from the rest of the country, not only geographically but also in terms of settlement patterns and level of economic development. This region is Turkey's "Wild East," a region of savage mountains jumbled together peak upon peak, of glacial lakes such as Lake Van—1,443 sq. mi. (3,738 sq. km.)—the country's largest, and of desolate plains leveling off toward the southeast. The Tigris and Euphrates rivers rise in eastern Anatolia and flow southeast toward the Persian Gulf, providing an enormous potential for irrigation and hydroelectric power that is only now beginning to be realized.

Eastern Anatolia is the ancestral homeland of two peoples who have played important roles in Anatolian history. They are the Kurds and the Armenians. Because of the rugged terrain, with agriculture possible only in a few deep fertile valleys, the principal economic activity has always been livestock raising. This region is prone to earthquakes and violent winters, with temperatures below −50°F (−45°C) not uncommon. The country's highest mountain, Mount Ararat (Ağri Dagı) is located here, straddling the border with Iran and the Soviet Union with its vast bulk and twin snow-capped peaks.

The republic's territory includes one other geographic region actually outside Anatolia. This region, the Hatay, occupies the extreme northeastern corner of the Mediterranean. (Our imaginative geographer would say

that it hangs down like the tail of the buffalo.) The Hatay has a large non-Turkish population—Syrian Arabs, Kurds, and others—and one hears as much Arabic and Kurdish as Turkish spoken on the streets of its cities. It was part of French-controlled Syria until 1938, when the population voted to join the Turkish Republic in a controversial referendum. It is an important region for the Turkish economy because of the port of Iskenderun, which, together with the new port of Mersin to the west, handles millions of tons of cargo annually, much of it as shipments of grain and winter vegetables to Europe and the Arab countries of the Middle East. A combination of efficient agricultural methods and irrigation has enabled Turkish farmers to produce three harvests a year in some areas, so these ports are always busy, and exports from them bring in much badly needed revenue.

Top left: Taken in 1890, this photo of Akhdamar shows pilgrims at the Armenian Apostolic Church of the Holy Cross. The Church of the Holy Cross, the main structure of a monastery complex, was built from 915–922 as the palace church of King Gagik Artzrouni; the adjacent building was built in the eighteenth century. Project SAVE/ Marie Bashian Bedikian/F.D. Green

Bottom left: A boat full of people leaving the island of Akhdamar in the middle of Lake Van. Joseph Lawton

Who Are the Turks?

Where a malignant and a turban'd Turk
Beat a Venetian and traduced the state . . .
Shakespeare, *Othello*, Act V, Scene II

How happy is the one who says "I am a Turk."
Mustafa Kemal Atatürk

The common mental image most Americans have of the Turks is probably closer to Shakespeare's description than to that of Turkey's twentieth-century national leader. It is an image of the "Terrible Turk," a turbaned warrior with huge ferocious mustaches, riding sword in hand through crowds of terrified Christian villagers, or a Barbary corsair with flaming red beard like that of Barbarossa, the terror of the Mediterranean in the sixteenth century, boarding helpless merchant ships to seize their gold and carry off the crew and any women aboard into slavery. Another traditional image of the Turk depicts a fat bejeweled sultan, lolling at his ease while eunuchs fan him and beautiful women belly dance for his pleasure. Women in this imagery are always veiled and secluded in a special section of the sultan's palace called the harem (an

Arabic word meaning "forbidden"), a place off limits to all men except their lord and master and male members of his immediate family.

To some extent these images, particularly the warrior ones, reflect the Turkish past. For over six centuries the Turks ruled nearly all of eastern Europe, seemingly unconquerable during much of that period. Partly out of fear, but also to stir up public patriotic sentiment, European rulers consciously promoted this ruthless, warlike image as a form of propaganda. As a result, the Balkan proverb "Grass never grows where a Turk's horse has trod" became widely popular and was taken for literal truth by Europeans as the image of the Turks.

In Italy the phrase "Mamma, gli Turchi!" ("Mamma, the Turks!") still survives in the Italian language from the days when Turkish corsairs harried coastal villages.

Such images, and memories preserved in European literature of the times when conquering Turkish armies stood at the gates of Vienna, still haunt the Turkish-European relationship.

Who are the Turks? How many of them are there? What makes them different from their neighbors? Is there such a thing as a specific *Turkish* physical type, something on which to hang a description, or characteristics of behavior that help to unite (or divide) them as a people? Answers to such questions help to explain better the inhabitants of this land that links Europe and Asia.

The population of Turkey in 1988 was over 55 million and growing nearly out of control. The birth rate presently stands at 2.4 percent annually. If this rate of increase continues, there will be 70–75 million Turks by the year A.D. 2000, putting a severe strain on the economy. Schools, hospital beds, jobs, and normal social services will somehow have to be provided for this booming population.

Street scene in modern Istanbul.   Richard Kalvar/Magnum

Other Turkish Peoples

Although they are a majority, the Turks in Turkey are not the only Turkish peoples in the world. There are large Turkish populations in the Soviet Union's Central Asian republics and in Zinjan Province, western China; and various tribes called Turkmen (Turkomans) are scattered throughout the Middle East. All of them speak various forms of the Turkish language that are as different from the Turkish spoken in the republic as English is from German. At one time in the early twentieth century Turkish leaders promoted a policy of "Pan-Turkism," the unity of all ethnically and linguistically related Turks into one nation. But modern Turkey does not subscribe to this policy. Other than concern for their general welfare as far-distant cousins, Turkey's Turks have little in common with other Turkish peoples.

Because Anatolia has been a land bridge for centuries, many different peoples have settled there and coexisted or intermarried. Consequently, one would be hard put to identify Turks on the basis of a set of physical characteristics. The crowds milling on the Galata Bridge on a summer evening, strolling along the waterfront in Izmir, or waiting in downtown Ankara for an *otobus* (bus) or *dolmuş* ("full"; a shared taxi, which takes people to various destinations and leaves when it is full), include a great variety of physical types. There are some whose blond hair and blue eyes suggest Scandinavian blood, stocky Mediterranean men with strong noses and women with black hair and black eyes, others with green or hazel eyes, even red-haired Turks, perhaps descended from the Crusaders who fought their ancestors on the way to the Holy Land. Some anthropologists believe that the only pure Turks are the Yürüks, a nomadic group found mostly in the Taurus Mountains. Their lifestyle resembles that of Gypsies; they speak an archaic form of Turkish and

Yürük

An American ambassador recalled: "I asked [a shepherd] what was a Yürük, a name often used synonymously with *nomad* in labeling rugs. He said a Yürük was a 'real' Turk. How can you tell? I asked. He said that Yürüks live in tents, not houses; they eat meat and cheese, not grain and vegetables; they raise animals, not crops; they are strong and courageous, not weak and timid. I went over the conversation later with several Turkish sociologists and historians. They said that the shepherd was right."

(James W. Spain, *American Diplomacy in Turkey*. New York: Praeger, 1984, p. 114.)

in stature and complexion might be said to resemble the short, swarthy warriors who rode out of Central Asia centuries ago.

The Turks are equally varied in their dress. No longer is there a specific type of costume that distinguishes them from each other. In the days before the republic, clothes were not only distinctive but also identified a person's social or economic status, family background, even occupation or profession. An American doctor who worked in Anatolia in the late 1800's wrote in his diary: "In the city the Turk wears a red fez, or a white turban if he were a teacher, a green one, if a descendant of the Prophet, or a small striped one, if an ordinary butcher or tanner or shopkeeper. White bloomers, with a long gown belted in with a handsome white girdle, completed his costume." (Alice Shepard Riggs, *Shepard of Aintab.* Boston: Interchurch Press, 1920, p. 32.)

This Turkish "high fashion" has disappeared. One of the reform efforts of Mustafa Kemal Atatürk in the early years of the republic was to encourage people to wear Western clothes as a sign of their modern thinking. As a result Turkey became for a while the world's largest market for secondhand clothing, much of it shipped from the garment district in New York!

Today, however, the well-dressed Turkish businessman wears Italian—or, increasingly, Turkish-made—suits, with white shirt and tie; female models display the latest fashions in coats and dresses (also Turkish-made) with styles rivaling those of Paris, while young people have adopted the universal costume of blue jeans and Reeboks. The one article of clothing left over from traditional times is the *şalvar,* loose baggy trousers commonly worn in the villages and in certain tourist towns such as the Mediterranean port of Alanya. However, many families keep their traditional costumes stored away and love to bring them out for holidays and festivals, wearing them with pride for the folk dances that often accompany such celebrations.

Regional Dances

Each region of Turkey has its own regional dances, handed down from generation to generation. The costumes worn at such dances vary from region to region but are always handmade; each item from shoes to cap or headdress is a work of the dressmaker's art. Socks, in particular, are woven in intricate patterns that can be "read" by those in the know to reveal hidden meanings. Many Turkish dances developed to celebrate the migration of villagers with their flocks from the village to the mountain pastures *(yayla)* in spring and summer. Turkish folk dancing has changed little in form over the centuries. Carved rock reliefs in Maraş, for example, depict women's costumes that are still worn by local women for the dances.

Origins of the Turks

The ancestors of the modern Turks apparently had no collective name for themselves, and no real sense of being a particular nation or people except in the attachment of related groups of families in the form of tribes. Their ancestral homeland is believed to have been in east-central Asia, in the area now occupied by the People's Republic of Mongolia. There they wandered and fought with other tribal peoples for the water and pasturage their flocks needed to survive in a hostile environment. They were people with no fixed address, living in black goat-hair tents called yurts, which are still used as homes by nomadic tribes in Asia and the deserts of the Middle East.

Turkish Language

Turkish is one of the languages of the Ural-Altaic linguistic group, and belongs to the Altaic branch of this group. The Altaic branch includes such diverse languages as Mongolian, Korean, and Japanese, along with various forms of Turkish (e.g. Uzbek, Kazakh) spoken in Soviet Central Asia. Turkish in these and other forms is the language of approximately 100 million people who inhabit a broad band of territory stretching from eastern Europe across Anatolia, northwest Iran, the Caucasus Mountains, and the Soviet Central Asian republics to the borders of China. However, due to the development of modern Turkish under the republic, the language differs significantly from that of other forms used elsewhere in this region. Its nearest equivalent is the Azeri dialect of the Turkish population of Azerbaijan, in northwest Iran.

During the Ottoman period Turkish was written in Arabic characters, from right to left, back to front in books and documents. Ottoman Turkish also borrowed heavily from other languages, and its use of many different forms of Arabic script made it incomprehensible to all except a few court officials and scribes. Atatürk was determined to provide his people with a usable language. He did away with Arabic letters, substituting a Latin alphabet with some letters modified to account for certain distinctly Turkish sounds. Most of the Arabic, Persian, and other loan words were purged and replaced by earlier Turkish ones, while words from European languages were borrowed and phoneticized in cases where no Turkish equivalent existed. Examples are *otomobil*, *tren*, *taksi*, *buro* (from the French *bureau*, "office").

These reforms have made modern Turkish relatively easy to

master. It has only one irregular noun, *su* ("water"), one irregular verb, *etmek* ("to be"), and no genders.

The alphabet consists of 29 letters: 21 consonants and 8 vowels. Six of these letters do not occur in English. They are: ç, ğ, ö, ş, ü, and the undotted i (ı). The English letters q, w, and x appear only in foreign words or phrases borrowed directly from other languages. Like all languages it lacks some sounds we think of as common: Turks learning English have difficulty with the pronunciation of the th in "Smith," for example, and with words that begin with "w."

The alphabet is as follows (as for any foreign language, equivalents are approximate):

a A	like the *u* in "gun"		m M	as in English
b B	as in English		n N	as in English
c C	like the *j* in "joke"		o O	like the *o* in "hope"
ç Ç	like the *ch* in "chin"		ö Ö	like the *ur* in "fur" or the *ir* in "bird"
d D	as in English			
e E	like the *e* in "pen"		p P	as in English
f F	as in English		r R	as in English
g G	as in "good"		s S	as in English
ğ Ğ	silent, serving to lengthen a preceding vowel		ş Ş	like the *sh* in "show" or the *s* in "sure"
h H	as in English		t T	as in English
ı I	like "ugh" or the *i* in "sir"		u U	like the *u* in "blue"
i I	like the *i* in "hit"		ü Ü	like the *ew* in "few" or feud
j J	like the *z* in "azure" or the *s* in "measure"		v V	as in English but rather soft, almost a *w*
k K	as in English		y Y	as in English
l L	as in English		z Z	as in English

Since Turkish has no genders, there is no distinction between he, she, and it, and no masculine-feminine classification of nouns. Turkish also has no articles: *Elma* can mean "apple," "the apple," or "an apple." The basic grammatical structure of sentences consists of subject-object-predicate (verb). Each word consists of a root form and one or more suffixes that denote place, action, possession, etc. The suffixes may also be added to nouns and verbs, so that sometimes a word gets long enough to become a whole sentence. The classic example is *Afyonkarahişarlılaştıramadiklarımızdanmuymuştınız*, meaning "Weren't you one of those people whom we tried unsuccessfully to make to resemble the citizens of Afyonkarahisar?"

The Turks are an extremely polite people—especially to visitors—and they use a large number of polite phrases and expressions in their daily conversation and everyday life. Here are some of them:

Hello	Merhaba	Mehr-hah-bah
Good morning/Good day	Gün aydın	Gew-nahy-duhn
Good evening	İyi akşamlar	E-yee ahk-shahm-lahr
Good night	Iyi geceler	E-yee geh-jeh-lehr
Good-bye (said by one leaving)	Allaha ısmarladık	Ah-lahs-mahr-lah-duhk
Good-bye (said by one staying)	Güle güle	Gew-leh gew-leh
How are you?	Nasılsınız?	Nahs-suhl-suh-nuhz
Very well	Çok iyiyim	Chohk e-yee-yeem
I'm fine	Iyiyim	E-yee-yeem
Thank you	Teşekkür ederim	Tesh-ek-kewr eh-dehr-eem
Pardon me	Affedersiniz	Ahf-feh-dehr-see-neez

May it contribute to your health! (said to one sitting down to a meal)	Afiyet olsun	Ah-fee-eht ohl-soon
Please	Lütfen	Lewt-fehn
May it last for hours! (said to one after a bath, a shave, or a haircut)	Saatler olsun!	Saaht-lehr ohl-soon
May your life be spared! (said when death mentioned)	Basınız sağ olsun!	Bah-shuh-nuhz saah ohl-soon
May your soul be spared! (said when something is broken)	Canınız sağ olsun!	Jah-nuh-nuz saah ohl-soon
May it be in the past! (said in cases of illness, injury, or distress)	Geçmis olsun!	Gech-meesh ohl-soon
To your health!	Şerefinize!	Sheh-rehf-ee-neez-eh

Lastly, the Turks use a good deal of "body language" in communicating among themselves and with others. For example, to say "yes" *(evet)* one nods the head forward and down, and to say "no" *(hayir)* one nods the head up and back. A more common form of "no" is simply to raise the eyebrows. A common (if somewhat rude) expression is *Yok*—literally, "it doesn't exist (here)," or "we don't have any," often encountered in shops; sometimes it is politely spoken, as in *"Yok, effendim"* ("we don't have any, sir"), but the customary usage is simply to raise the eyebrows heavenward and purse the lips to make a sound like "tsk." Visitors who don't understand this "silent language" can spend a lot of time in shops waiting for the proprietor to answer questions!

Language was the major link between these as yet unnamed peoples. Tablets discovered in the late nineteenth century in the Orkhon basin of Russian Central Asia (the so-called "Orkhon inscriptions") provide the earliest evidence to date of the particular language known today as Turkish. These inscriptions date back to the seventh and eighth centuries A.D. Already by that time various Turkish-speaking tribes had migrated westward from their homelands, driven by the constant need for water and pasturage and often in conflict with other, non-Turkish tribes competing for the same territory. Eventually their migrations brought them into the northern regions of the Middle East, into Iran, Mesopotamia (Iraq), and the vast plains of Anatolia.

In their wanderings these Turkish-speaking peoples moved from a pastoral semidesert environment into one of settled villages and towns with a long-established civilization. The first significant transformation in the lives of the Turks was the adoption of the principal written language of the region, Arabic. The Arabic language, originally also a simple one, had developed an elaborate grammar and script through contact with other languages, notably Greek, Latin, and Farsi (Persian). The Arabic language adopted many loan words from these languages. Because it was the language of a dominant religion, it became the language of business and commerce, government and social relations, in the region. Mastery of Arabic was the key to technology, science, mathematics, philosophy, even medicine. The linguistic adaptability of the Turks, along with their military skills, enabled them to advance rapidly toward success in the new world they had entered.

Islam, the Dominant Religion

Along with a new language the Turks acquired a new religion. It was and still is the dominant faith in a vast area, from northern Africa as far as northern India, Indonesia, and the Philippines, and with millions of members in other parts of the world, including the United States. This religion, called Islam, is one of three major world religions based on belief in one God. By virtue of their conversion to Islam the Turks became members of a worldwide community of believers.

In Arabic *Islam* means "submission" in the sense of submission to God (or the will of God). Those who "submit" are known as Muslims. As noted, it is a monotheistic religion, centered upon the belief in one God (Allah in Arabic), a belief that it shares under different names with Judaism and Christianity. But Islam is younger in age, having begun as an organized religion in the seventh century A.D. Muslims believe that Islam began as a series of revelations from God, via the Angel Gabriel, to a man named Muhammad, a merchant who lived in the city of Mecca, in southwestern Arabia. The revelations were received by Muhammad orally over a period of several years, and he passed them on directly to his listeners and followers. Eventually they were written down in Arabic in a book, the Koran, which Muslims believe is literally the Word of God.

Muslims do not believe in Jesus as the Son of God. They believe that Allah is One, unique and indivisible. This difference in belief is one factor in the long history of conflict between Christians and Muslims over the centuries. Yet Islam has proven itself to be a more tolerant religion over the centuries than has Christianity in many respects. Traditionally, in areas where Islamic power dominated, Christian communities were allowed to live largely unmolested under the protection of Muslim rulers and to practice their religion. However, they were charged a special tax while under Muslim rule, and in times of unrest or weak rulers they often came under attack by Muslim mobs. In terms of theology Muslims practice what theologians call radical monotheism; that is, God is not divisible into parts. In this respect Islam is closer to Judaism than it is to Christianity.

Muslims have a high regard for Jesus as a holy man, a miracle worker, and a prophet in the long line of biblical prophets stretching back in time to Moses and Abraham. Muslims do not worship Muhammad as divine, but they believe he was the "seal of the prophets," the last messenger to receive and transmit God's revelations to humankind. As a result they believe that the lives of Muhammad and, by extension, that of his family would serve as ideal role models for their own lives.

Islam began its fourteenth century of existence in 1979. It was originally an Arab religion exclusively: God's word was revealed to Muhammad in his own language, and the first Muslims were Arabs from Mecca and other Arabian cities and towns. But in his last sermon before his death, in A.D. 632, Muhammad preached a message of universal brotherhood (and sisterhood), citing a revelation that "every Muslim is a brother unto every other Muslim, and ye are all one brotherhood." Fired up by these words, Muslim missionaries struck out in all directions to expand the faith, aided by swift-moving Arab armies, and before long a great variety of non-Arab peoples had been converted to Islam.

Islam provides a total way of life for its followers, from cradle to grave. It is also a relatively simple faith to live by. All that is required for a person to become a Muslim is to state that he or she believes in Allah and in Muhammad as the Messenger of Allah, and to follow five basic rules of conduct. These rules are usually called the Five Pillars because they "support" or hold up the "House" of Islam.

Although Islam is a single community, without the denominations that exist in Christianity, a difference of opinion developed early regarding leadership. Muhammad had barely established the community when he died unexpectedly, at age sixty-two. Like most of us he was not ready to die. He was still enjoying the flush of success against his enemies in Mecca, and had made no provisions for the future of the small Muslim community. He had made no will, no arrangements that we know of for a successor to carry on his work. Nor were there any instructions in the Koran to guide his perplexed and grieving followers.

In their dilemma the Muslims decided on a successor in traditional tribal fashion: They elected the oldest and wisest member of the community—the second convert after Muhammad's wife, his father-in-law—as Caliph, literally the "agent" or deputy of the Messenger of God. A series of caliphs presided over Islam's swift expansion from a small corner of Arabia into a world empire. The caliphs combined spiritual and temporal authority. Despite frequent changes in location and line of descent, the office of Caliph served to unite Muslims until well into the twentieth century.

Most Muslims accept this sequence of events: Muhammad's death, the election of a Caliph, the establishment of a global Islamic empire, the present division of the Islamic world into nation-states, as foreordained in accordance with Allah's will. They are known as "Sunni" Muslims because they observe the *Sunna*, the sacred "way" of Islam defined in the Koran; the teachings of Muhammad; the line of caliphs;

The Five Pillars of Islam

1. Confession of Faith—"I testify that there is no God but Allah, and that Muhammad is the Messenger of God."
2. Prayer, obligatory five times daily, always facing in the direction of Mecca.
3. Fasting during the lunar month of Ramadan (Ramazan in Turkish), the month of the first revelations. The fast is obligatory for Muslims during the daylight hours of the entire month.
4. Alms giving or tithing.
5. Pilgrimage, at least once in one's lifetime, to the holy cities of Mecca and Medina (where Muhammad died and is buried).

and the sequence of Islamic history. But a significant minority rejects this historical progression as being contrary to what God, and Muhammad, had intended. (They do observe the Sunna, however.) This minority is known as the *Shia*, an Arabic word meaning "partisans." The Shia are "Partisans of Ali"; they believe that Muhammad had intended to name Ali, his first cousin and the husband of his only surviving daughter, as his successor, but died before he could do so. The Shia contend that the right to leadership in the Islamic community is a divine right bestowed on Muhammad and his immediate family by Allah. It can only be inherited by his direct descendants.

The main difference between Sunnis and Shias concerns belief in leadership. The Shia consider the descendants of Muhammad through Ali and his sons, and particularly the younger son Hussein, as their imams or spiritual leaders. When the last Imam supposedly died in the ninth century (probably of poison), leading Shia scholars said he was not dead but hidden (alive, present in the world but invisible) and would return at the end of time to pronounce the Day of Judgment. Until then the Shia religious leaders would provide leadership for the community, interpret God's will in accordance with their powers of intercession and insight, and serve as "Supreme Guides" in the decision-making process.

Over the centuries two other factors have emerged that affect the modern Sunni-Shia relationship. One is the rise of a Shia center of power in Iran as a rival to Sunni authority. The other factor in the Sunni-Shia conflict results from economic and social discrimination against Shias by Sunnis. This has not been a persistent problem in Turkey, but in other Islamic countries Shias have been deprived of voting rights, education, and other opportunities.

The majority of Turks are Sunni Muslims, but there is a significant Shia minority, 20 percent according to some estimates. Turkey's Shias are known as Alevis, the Turkish equivalent of Partisans of Ali. They tend to support the government in its separation of religion from the state, and consider themselves loyal citizens. Only one political party in recent years, the Unity Party (formed in 1966) had a predominately Alevi membership. In the period of the Ottoman Empire Shias were distrusted and discriminated against, sometimes persecuted for their presumed loyalty to Iranian Shia rulers. But the only significant case of Sunni-Alevi conflict in recent history was a riot in December 1978 in the southeastern city of Kahramanmaraş, which has a large Alevi population. Alevi neighborhoods were invaded by right-wing terrorists in their campaign to bring down the government, and battles developed that split along Sunni-Alevi lines.

Other Ethnic Groups

The Kurds form a separate group within the Muslim population. They are an ancient people springing from diverse origins, but over the centuries they have developed a distinct culture and strong social cohesion. Turkey's Kurds are part of a much larger Kurdish population spread over the mountains of eastern Anatolia, northern Iraq, Syria, and western Iran, their traditional homeland. There are no reliable surveys of the Kurdish population either in Turkey or in these neighboring countries. Estimates for Turkey's Kurds range from 2.5 million to 7.5 million, which would be 14 percent of the total population.

The Kurds of Turkey are Sunni Muslims like the majority of their Turkish compatriots. But their language, culture, and historical traditions are quite different. Kurdish is a separate language from Turkish, derived from Indo-European origins. It is related to Farsi (Persian), although different in grammar and vocabulary, and is written in Arabic letters, another difference from modern Turkish. (One reason for the difficulty in obtaining accurate census data on the Kurds is that many

Kurdish saddlemakers, metalworkers, and weavers line the streets of Urfa.
Sharon Guynup

of them also speak Turkish and are therefore not counted in the Kurdish population.)

Kurds are by tradition fiercely independent, and are tightly organized at the village or clan level. But they have never developed into a unified nation or a separate national state, always being ruled by others. During the Ottoman period the government preferred to rule them indirectly through tribal overlords, mainly because conquest and direct control would have been very difficult in the inaccessible Kurdish mountains.

The government of the Turkish republic was more interested in establishing a homogeneous, unified Turkish nation than in preserving the status and rights of the minorities, both Muslim and non-Muslim, that had existed in Ottoman times. A Kurdish rebellion against Atatürk in the 1920's was crushed ruthlessly, and from then on successive

Turkish governments largely ignored them. Some officials and intellectuals even claimed that the Kurds were really "mountain Turks" who had lost their language and forgotten their origins.

The changes that have affected Turkish society generally in the late twentieth century have also been felt by the Kurds. Previously they kept to themselves in their mountain villages, scratching a meager living from small plots cultivated along the steep slopes and traveling with their flocks of sheep and goats from lowland meadows to high upland pastures for winter and summer pasturage. Otherwise they rarely left their villages and had little knowledge of the outside world. Today more and more Kurds are migrating to towns and cities elsewhere in Turkey, part of the general movement from rural to urban areas that is changing Turkey's society. The majority work as porters, sanitation workers, waiters and in other menial occupations, but increasingly young Kurds are finding their way to schools and urban universities to pursue education for professional careers.

For the Kurds who remain in the hills, life is difficult; eastern Turkey is still the country's most impoverished region. Kurdish leaders have long felt that the government does not care about them because they are somehow "different"; it continues to ignore their needs for education, job opportunities, roads, and public services. In the 1970's a Kurdish nationalist movement emerged to press these demands through political violence. One faction, the Kurdish Workers' Party, even demanded a separate Kurdish state. Although the movement was ruthlessly repressed after the 1980 military coup, continued clashes between government forces and Kurdish guerrillas finally forced the new civilian government in the 1980's to take Kurdish demands seriously. A large-scale development program got under way in areas of Kurdish settlement, and in 1987 the teaching of Kurdish language and literature in Kurdish schools was permitted as a recognition of a separate Kurdish culture. The government also allowed some 100,000 Kurdish refugees fleeing persecution and poison gas attacks in neighboring Iraq to resettle in Turkey.

The Non-Muslim Population

Modern Turkey has several small non-Muslim minority groups left over from the multi-ethnic population of the Ottoman empire. There are about 21,000 Jews; the majority of the country's Jewish population of over 200,000 emigrated to Israel when that state was established in 1948. The remaining Jews are protected under law and have the right to practice their religion freely guaranteed under the constitution of the republic. Several years ago the main Jewish synagogue in Istanbul was badly damaged by a terrorist bomb, and a number of worshipers were killed or injured. The congregation's Muslim neighbors immediately took up a collection and formed work parties to help repair the building.

The Greeks, a larger non-Muslim group, formed a large percentage of the Ottoman population. But after the republic was formed, the vast majority of the Greeks living in Anatolia and eastern Thrace were exchanged for a comparable Turkish population in western Thrace, now a part of Greece. Although the remaining Greeks live under the protection of Turkish laws and have the right to practice their religion freely, there are clear and ever-present tensions between the two governments.

The world headquarters of the Greek Orthodox Church is in Istanbul. The head of this church, the Patriarch, is a Turkish citizen and travels on a Turkish passport, even if engaged in evangelism or in trying to bring about the unity of the Eastern and Roman Catholic churches.

The Samele monastery has not been used for religious purposes for over sixty years, but tourists now wend their way up the mountain to visit it. Joseph Lawton

The Armenian community of Harput assembles to greet the bride and groom of the Zouloumian family in 1892. Project SAVE/Ardashess Hampar

The Armenians

The Armenians, today a small Christian minority group largely confined to Istanbul, played an important role in Anatolia in the past. They trace their origin to ancient times and, like the Kurds, have an identification with a particular homeland in the eastern part of the peninsula and the mountains around Mount Ararat. Although from ancient times many of them lived in this area, under Turkish rule Armenians formed the majority of the population in the eastern provinces.

They were primarily villagers, but towns and cities throughout Anatolia also had flourishing communities of Armenian artisans and traders. A relatively high level of education (fostered by the Armenian church, traditionally a source of strength for Armenian identity and national feeling) enabled a number of Armenians to become influential in the economic and financial affairs of the Ottoman Turkish government. This was particularly true in the nineteenth century, when European countries began to dominate the Turkish economy as well as its internal politics, and European ideas of liberty and equality circulated among the non-Muslim subject peoples. However, efforts by Armenian intellectuals to gain better treatment for the mass of the Armenian people, who lived under constant threat of repression by the Turkish government as well as persecution by Muslim mobs, had the opposite effect. In 1895–96 the government became convinced the Armenians were disloyal and carried out a series of frightful massacres. Further massacres took place during World War I, this time because the government viewed the Armenians as a potential source of disloyalty because of contacts with Russia, which was then at war with Turkey. By the 1920's over two million Armenians had been killed, been deported, or fled into exile. The Armenian question remains a dark chapter in Turkey's relations with the world, especially as the present Turkish government consistently refuses to acknowledge any responsibility for its predecessor's treatment of the Armenians.

Modern Turkish Society

The long and rich history of Anatolia, the heritage of its ancient civilizations, the merging of different peoples, and a variety of cultural influences form the base for modern Turkish society. The long period of

Ottoman rule as a multinational state blended cultural influences, so one cannot say there is a clear-cut Turkish type. There are, however, uniting influences, the most important of these being Islam.

Islam continues to unite the nation, despite disagreement as to the extent of its domination over personal life. The modern Turkish language, purged of most of its loan words, also creates a sense of national solidarity. Mustafa Kemal Atatürk, who judged the temperament of the people well, saw them as dour, conservative, fatalistic, stubborn, and patient. Obviously such qualities will vary from person to person, from place to place, and in relation to family background, education, and economic or social status. Turks will often disagree violently in matters of politics, and although Islam has become a personal matter for most of them, such questions as female modesty of dress, use of alcohol or wine, boy-girl relations, and public displays of affection cause considerable friction, both between parents and young people and between traditional and modern-minded Muslims.

In 1988 the government passed a law prohibiting the wearing of headscarves by female students in university classes in an effort to discourage Islamic fundamentalists who insisted that Islam required them to be worn in public.

Several qualities seem to be widely shared among Turks. They are hospitable and generous to a fault, fiercely proud, and deeply attached to their families. Turkish hospitality is proverbial—the guest in a village home is given the place of honor and generously fed regardless of the family's economic circumstances. The proverb "A visitor comes with ten blessings, eats one, and leaves nine" is not taken lightly.

The Turkish family is usually a close-knit one, with parents taking great pride in their children. Turkey is one of the few countries in the world that has a national holiday for children (April 23). On this day it is the custom for each family to outfit the children with new clothes; if they cannot afford them, the town will help provide them.

Turkish pride arises out of its past, and from the nation's ability to rise from defeat and remake itself into a modern democratic republic. Its democracy admittedly has imperfections, but the effort to build continues. The motto engraved on the Workers' Monument in Ankara, taken from an Atatürk slogan, aptly describes this modern Turkish spirit:

> Oğun! Çalis! Güven!
> Be proud! Work! Be confident!

As the century nears its final decade, the Turks are hard at work fulfilling these prescriptions.

The Weight of the Past

Lend me the stone strength of the past and I will lend you
The wings of the future, for I have them.

Robinson Jeffers, *To the Rock That Will Be a Cornerstone*

Civilization in Anatolia dates back more than ten thousand years. Already by 7000 B.C. the peninsula had been settled by small groups of people who had changed their lifestyle from that of hunters living in caves to become farmers growing crops of barley and beans, and who clustered together in houses of mud brick. The oldest permanent settlement yet discovered, anywhere on earth, is Çatalhöyük. It is located about thirty miles south of Konya, in the dead center of Anatolia, and dates back to the 7th millennium B.C.! Today there is nothing to see in Çatalhöyük except a mound and the outlines of a few buildings. The pottery, skulls, bones, simple tools, and utensils dug up by archaeologists are in a museum in Ankara. But the past weighs heavily here as one climbs to the top of the mound and looks out over the dusty plain. It is easy to imagine people going about their business, planting, harvesting, cooking, meeting friends and neighbors in the streets of Çatalhöyük almost at the beginning of civilization.

Another Anatolian settlement, somewhat newer, which is now being excavated, has begun to change our thinking about early humans. This settlement, Cayonu, is located inland, not far from the headwaters of the Tigris River. In 7000 B.C. Cayonu had a resident population of 500. Its residents also lived in mud-brick houses, but the bricks were mortared with a mixture of plaster and straw so that they could withstand heavy rains. Cayonu's people cultivated garden plots of wheat and legumes and made fine tools—kitchen implements, knives, pins, and hooks— out of copper from a nearby copper mine that is still in use.

But the real surprise for the archaeologists excavating Cayonu was its urban layout and the level of technology attained by its residents. It has the world's first identifiable community center, where citizens would gather to discuss civic problems, hold social events, or celebrate the festivals of the agricultural calendar. One of the center's buildings still has a floor made of terrazzo, a construction technique erroneously thought to have been invented by the Romans many centuries later. This floor is of salmon-colored limestone and marble chips put together by a technique we call pyrotechnology. This involves burning limestone to make cement, with the marble chips set in the mixture while it is soft and hot. Other floors in the excavated complex are made of flagstones set in cement, fitted together perfectly and looking as if they were laid yesterday.

Cities and Empires

These early Anatolian settlements were small, not more than a few hundred people. But as the agriculture improved and settlements became organized politically, they grew into cities. The first people in the region to extend their rule over a large area and to underscore their authority by building cities were the Hittites, who developed a powerful

Hittite-era art: typical sunburst shape with stag, found at Alacahöyük. It dates from about 2300–2100 B.C.   Ankara Archaeological Museum

empire during the Bronze Age (2600–1200 B.C.). The Hittites stood on equal terms with the Egyptians, the major power of that time. Yet until recently very little was known about them. The first clues to their existence—and importance—were unearthed by a Frenchman, Charles Texier, who was wandering about Anatolia in the 1830's looking for other ruined cities. Near the village of Boğazköy, 120 miles (193 km.) from Ankara, the villagers told him about some huge stone carvings lying about on a nearby ridge. Texier struggled up a rough cart track to the crest of the ridge, and found himself in the middle of what had obviously been a large city at one time. It was nearly a mile long, encircled by the remains of massive walls made of unmortared granite blocks. Many of the blocks had raised carvings of lions, winged monsters, and humans on them. The Frenchman was amazed. He had never seen such people—short stocky bodies, broad flat foreheads, huge hooked noses. As he traced the outlines of the city, it seemed to him that only a wealthy and powerful nation could have built it. Yet he knew of no such nation in Anatolia's early past.

We know now that Texier had discovered the capital city of the Hittites, Hattusa (or Hattusas, derived from the original builders, the Hatti.) Excavations were delayed for many years due to political instability and lack of access to the site. They began in 1905, and among other archaeological treasures uncovered were the Hittite state archives, some 2,500 clay tablets. Many of them were inscribed in an unknown hieroglyphic language, others in the Babylonian cuneiform characters commonly used in the Near East at that time. In 1915 an Austrian scholar deciphered them through brilliant detective work: He compared the hieroglyphic signs with the cuneiform characters to give our modern world a clear picture of this mysterious people. The tablets provide much useful information, such as the fact that only Hittite kings and nobles were allowed to eat fish or meat; the lower classes lived on bread, honey, cheese, vegetables, and fruit.

The modern Turks like to include the Hittites among their ancestors, although the connection is very doubtful. *Arslan*, the Turkish word for "lion," is a common first or last name in Turkey today. But the Hittites had other skills besides lionlike courage. They were great builders and brilliant military strategists. They developed the two-man chariot with open spoked wheels into a superior offensive weapon. Hittite charioteers and bowmen fought the powerful Egyptian army to a draw in the battle of Kadesh (1298 B.C.). The ensuing treaty between them set a standard that has not been bettered by twentieth-century negotiators.

Hattusa was the first Hittite city to be discovered, but others were soon located in the same area, such as Alacahöyük, Karatepe, Kultepe, and Yazilikaya. The last named proved to be the Hittite national religious sanctuary. Yazilikaya was filled with shrines to various Hittite gods and goddesses, some sixty-six of them; inscriptions on their effigies list their names and their particular roles, which are usually associated with some natural force such as wind, rain, or sun. But the most beguiling thing about this Hittite sculpture is its humanness. A frieze from Hattusa, for example, has a boy playing with his pet lamb, a girl with a whirligig, bearded envoys bringing gifts to a King. There is even a flat rock with the Hittite words for "school rock," possibly indicating a long-vanished school where children learned their lessons thirty centuries ago.

The Mound of Troy

The Hittite empire eventually fell into decline. Hattusa was abandoned and ravaged by fire, and new power centers developed as other migrating peoples moved into Anatolia. Often they built new urban centers on top of existing cities, layer upon layer. The city park in Konya, for example, is built over a mound covering the remains of settlements that date back to the Bronze Age.

The most interesting example of this layering process may be seen in the far northwest corner of the peninsula, where a flat-topped mound dominates the rolling countryside of grain fields and scattered villages. A small sign identifies the mound simply as "Truva." Truva is the Turkish word for Troy, according to legend one of the great cities of ancient Anatolia. The blind poet Homer, in his epic poem *The Iliad,* told the story of the ten-year siege of Troy by the Greeks, which ended in the destruction of the city. Homer lived many centuries after this supposed event took place, and whether he was telling the tale of the siege as it had been handed down from generation to generation or adding drama to a simple legend is not known. There is some question as to whether Homer ever existed; some scholars believe *The Iliad* was the work of a number of epic storytellers.

Whatever the facts—and in Anatolia legend is often intermingled with fact—when archaeologists began digging in the ruins of Troy, they found not one but nine cities, each one built on top of the previous one. All together the nine cities span nearly four thousand years. None of them were very large, suggesting a minor battle rather than a ten-year siege that supposedly changed the course of history and opened the way for the spread of Greek civilization across the peninsula and throughout the Mediterranean area. But there is an atmosphere about this windy plain, with its ring of tumbled walls and ruined buildings, that lets the legend of Troy speak for itself. On a clear day one can see the blue line of the Straits, the funnels of passing ships, and it is not difficult to imagine the Greek triremes (war ships) drawn up on shore, the dust spiraling up from Achilles's chariot as he dragged the dead Hector, Troy's hero, three times around the walls. The modern Turks have built a huge replica of the wooden horse that the Greeks used, according to Homer, to hide warriors, allowing them to get inside the walls and end the siege.

Legendary Characters

The ancient Anatolian past is filled with stories of unusual characters, some perhaps based upon real persons, whose names and lives have become part of our literature and folklore. One of them was Gordius, who began his life as a farmer and ended it as a King. He lived in an area ruled by the Phrygians, successors to the Hittites.

The Phrygian elders wanted a King because they needed someone to mediate their quarrels, and also because having a King would give them status with their neighbors. They asked the local oracle (the fortune-

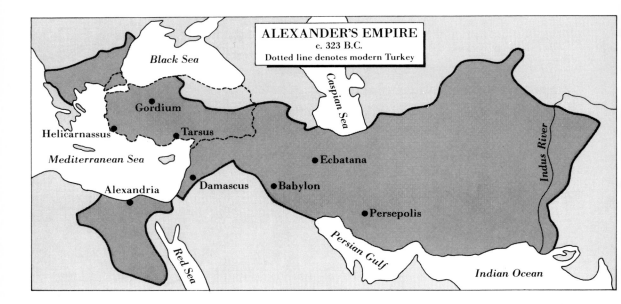

teller of that time) for his advice. "Watch for the first person to pass my shrine riding in a cart," thundered the oracle, "and he will be your king. You can't do any better." The elders rushed out to the road, and there was Gordius in his oxcart on his way to market. In this curious fashion he became their king.

Gordius had another claim to fame, however. He was very proud of the fittings on his oxcart, particularly the knot that tied the pole of the cart to the axle tree, because it was an unusually intricate one. He had designed it himself, and he used to challenge passersby to untie it. But no one could. The obliging oracle then predicted that the first person to untie the knot would rule over all of Asia. Long after Gordius had died, the cart stood there with its knot in the middle of his capital city, Gordium, hurling a perpetual challenge at all potential unknotters. At last Alexander the Great passed through Gordium on his way to fight the Persians, rulers of much of Asia at that time. Alexander studied the knot, and then simply cut it in two with a slice of his sword. Then he went on to conquer most of Asia. So "cutting the Gordian knot" has come into modern English as an expression of how one solves a difficult problem in a direct but unexpected way.

Gordius's most important successor as ruler of the Phrygians was King Midas, who ruled about 2,700 years ago. Midas, it is said, had an unusual talent: He could turn anything he touched into gold—including his daughter, as he discovered one evening to his eternal regret when he gave her a fatherly hug. Thanks to King Midas the "Midas touch" (or the "golden touch") has become another common expression; we use it for persons who seem to have a knack for making money.

A Parade of Invaders

Other ancient peoples followed the Hittites, migrating into Anatolia, intermingling, sometimes absorbed or conquered by more vigorous groups in an endless flow of human activity. Long before the Turks arrived, these various peoples had built up the base of Anatolian civilizations. The Lycians, for example, moving into a rugged corner along the southwest coast, carved magnificent tombs in the cliffs that fall sheer into the Mediterranean, causing us to marvel at their engineering skill. The Lydians, another important people, were, as far as is known, the first people to use coin money in their transactions. From their capital, Sardis, on the Pactolus River, they controlled the major east-west and north-south trade routes across the peninsula. In order to inspire confidence in the merchants and caravan traders they dealt with, by giving them something permanent and of value, they made metal discs, which were usually stamped with a figure of a lion or a fox. Gradually Lydian discs became legal tender throughout the Mediterranean, laying the foundation for the modern system of currency exchange.

Phrygians

Little was known about the Phrygians or their golden ruler until the 1950's, when archaeologists began excavating a huge mound near the village of Yassihöyük, southwest of Ankara, on the chance that it might hide the ruins of Gordium. They "struck gold" as a result, finding not only the remains of the Phrygian capital but several tombs of royalty, one eventually identified as the tomb of Midas. It contained among other relics a collection of fine wood furniture. The beautifully made boxwood tables, inlaid with juniper, and serving trays carved in intricate geometric designs, revealed the high quality of Phrygian craftsmanship. However, when the furniture was removed to the Hittite Museum in Ankara, it began to deteriorate rapidly; burial in the earthen mound had preserved it for more than two thousand years, but the pollutants in the air threatened to undo years of archaeological work.

Fortunately the new understanding of wood chemistry developed in recent years has enabled archaeologists to preserve wooden items that would otherwise have disintegrated. The Midas furniture was impregnated with polyvinyl butyral and Acryloid, and then sprayed with Rutapox, an epoxy resin, to hold the fibers in place. Thanks to modern technology, one can dine at King Midas's table as agreeably as he did long ago.

Hellenism

Some time between the thirteenth and twelfth centuries B.C., Greek colonization of Asia Minor began in earnest. Greek cities sprang up everywhere on the peninsula, but especially in the west and south and along the coasts. Some of these cities were built high in the mountains as defensive strongholds, while others developed around natural harbors, trade crossroads, or shrines to oracles, gods, or goddesses. Greek settlement linked Anatolia and its nearby islands with mainland Greece by a common language, culture, literature, philosophy, art, and democratic tradition. Greek cities on the peninsula duplicated those on the mainland in their grid design, with a central complex of law courts, municipal buildings, theater, temples, and streets at right angles from the center. Although political power passed into alien hands—Persian, Macedonian, and ultimately Roman—the predominant influence in western and central Anatolia remained Greek.

However, in eastern Anatolia a different civilization slowly took shape. One of the city-states that had emerged from the breakup of the Hittite empire was Urartu, populated originally by various migrating peoples, including the Phrygians. Urartu was an important state for several centuries because of its control over trade routes leading from the Mediterranean through the Caucasus Mountains and eastward into Iran and central Asia. Thus, there was much interchange between the people of Urartu and the Greeks to the west as well as Persians to the east.

Urartu gradually disappeared as a political entity as other rulers and foreign powers won control of Anatolia. However, out of the mixture of peoples that made up the Urartian population, there emerged a distinctive group, the Armenians, with a separate language and culture. Their principal area of settlement was the highlands around Mount Ararat, and, although they were ruled by others, they maintained a distinctive identity and a close-knit village life.

In the second century B.C. Artaxias, an Armenian general in the service of the Seleucid dynasty then in power in Anatolia, declared his independence and established the kingdom of Greater Armenia.

Artaxias played an important part in the history of his people because he not only defined Armenia's borders in an area that Armenians today still regard as their true homeland, but also promoted the use of the Armenian language at his court.

Artaxias's great-grandson, Tigranes (95–55 B.C.), extended the boundaries of Greater Armenia southward to Cilicia on the Mediterranean coast of Anatolia, and as far as Phoenicia (modern Lebanon). For this reason he is referred to by Armenians as "The Great." Armenia was an important power in his time, and Armenian settlement and culture became prominent in a broad area reaching from the sea to the Caucasus Mountains.

The Power of Rome

Rome had already become the major power in the western Mediterranean after defeating its great rival, Carthage, in the third century B.C. In the second and first centuries B.C. the Romans moved east, taking advantage of rivalries among various Greek and other princes to bring Anatolia and eventually the entire Middle East under their control. In Anatolia they found a somewhat unusual way to divide and rule: The King of Pergamum had signed a treaty with Rome that stipulated that in return for aid against his rivals, he would bequeath his kingdom to Rome if he or any of his successors died without heirs. Attalus III met this requirement, and at his death the kingdom of Pergamum became the Roman province of Asia.

Roman Remains

Rome gave the peoples of the peninsula an efficient administration, Roman law, good roads, public security, and the protection of the

Great Diana of the Ephesians, a statue of Artemis (Diana) from the Roman period. Izmir Archaeological Museum

The remains of the Roman library at Ephesus.   Turkish Tourism Office

Pergamum

Pergamum was famous for its library and medical school and for
the invention of parchment, an early writing material made from
animal hides instead of the papyrus reeds used in Egypt. The city
also had probably the first medical clinic where psychology was
used as a healing device. Patients were told to walk through a
vaulted underground corridor toward the temple of Telesphorus, one
of the gods of medicine. As they walked along, voices called
incantations and mystical verses down to them through openings in
the vaulted ceiling. If that did not work, they could sleep in the
temple and hope that Telesphorus would send a diagnosis and
perhaps a cure to them in a dream.

Roman legions. The Romans also improved on Greek cities, so much
so that it is difficult to tell where one ends and the other begins in the
ruined sites that may be found today in nearly every corner of Turkey.
The country has over forty thousand documented Greco-Roman historical sites, more Greek sites than there are in Greece, more Roman sites
than in Italy, but barely one percent have been excavated. Dig almost
anywhere in any farmer's field, any outcropping or mound, and frag-
ments of pottery, coins, bits of statuary or other artifacts come to light.

Christianity and "New Rome"

Anatolia figured large in the development of Christianity in the Roman
Empire. Tarsus, today an insignificant town, was the home of Saul, a
Roman citizen and Jew who changed from persecutor of the new Chris-

tian faith to its greatest advocate after his conversion experience on the road to Damascus. As the Apostle Paul, he preached his first sermon in Perge on the the Mediterranean coast, defying the pagan Roman gods worshiped by its citizens.

A greater challenge awaited Paul in Ephesus, at that time a seaport and the richest city in Asia Minor. The people of Ephesus worshiped the goddess Diana, whose temple was considered to be one of the Seven Wonders of the ancient world. The silversmiths of Ephesus were famous for their skill, deriving a good income from the sale of small silver models of the temple to visitors and pilgrims.

When Paul began preaching, they hooted him down, forcing him out of the theater by throwing stones at him. The Ephesians then marched along the Sacred Way shouting, "Great is Diana of the Ephesians." It must have been quite a scene. But in time the opposition died away, the Ephesians were converted to the new faith, and the city became the seat of a bishop.

Ephesus is associated with Christianity in another way. About three miles out of town is a small chapel built on the site of a house said to be the last earthly home of the Virgin Mary, whom the Turks call Meryemana. It is believed by some that after the crucifixion of Jesus, Mary was entrusted to the care of the Disciple John and accompanied him to Ephesus, where she died. Her reputed burial site is nearby.

The Byzantine Empire, Rome Extended

The last act in Anatolia's pre-Turkish past was a long one, lasting about a thousand years. Late in the fourth century A.D. the Roman Empire was divided into two roughly equal parts, each ruled by an emperor. The Eastern Roman Empire corresponded to what is today the Middle East (excluding Iran). It included the modern states of Turkey, Syria, Jordan, Israel, Egypt, and Iraq, although Iraq was ruled partly by the Romans

The small chapel in Meryemana, reputed to be the last home of the Virgin Mary.   Turkish
Information Office

and partly by the Persians. The division of the empire was made in
order to meet the invasion of its frontiers by barbarian tribes more
efficiently, but the two emperors ruled as equals.

The western half of the empire was still ruled from Rome, but the
eastern emperor made his headquarters in the ancient Greek city of
Byzantium. For this reason the empire is usually referred to as the
Byzantine Empire. However, its capital was renamed Constantinople in
A.D. 330 in honor of the Emperor Constantine, who made Christianity
the official religion of the entire Roman Empire. Following Constantine's example, the Eastern Roman Emperors called themselves "Vicars
of Christ on Earth," claiming responsibility for the defense of the faith

and spiritual authority over all Christians.

The base of Byzantine power was Anatolia. The peninsula and Egypt were the main sources of the empire's agricultural wealth, contributing grain, timber, gold, and other resources to the economy. Anatolia was also the principal source of manpower for the empire's armies and fleet. Wealthy nobles and military leaders were often given large estates in Anatolia in return for services to the emperor. These nobles were required to send at least one family member to Constantinople to enter the emperor's service.

Although they functioned as independent monarchs in their own lands, the nobles were intensely loyal to their emperor, whom they revered as Christ's representative on earth. In times of crisis it was not unusual to see a noble arriving in Constantinople with an entire regiment of retainers, flags waving and armor glittering in the sun as they rode through the city streets.

Life in Byzantine Anatolia was harder for the lower classes, but it was still bearable. Most farmers owned their own land, worked it, bought livestock on credit, and lived in houses filled with relatives. But there were always rural pleasures, weddings, and other family celebrations to look forward to. Travelers from Constantinople would often stop long enough to enjoy Anatolian hospitality and to delight their hosts with tales of the great city, "like a young girl, bedecked with gold and precious stones." Most families had sons in the army, and when they came home, there were more stories to tell of chivalrous Arabs on the eastern front or barbarian Bulgars amid the pine forests north toward Russia.

The Queen of Cities remained a glittering prize that lay temptingly beyond the reach of her many enemies. Siege after siege failed to break through her massive walls. Within those walls was wealth and beauty

Interior of Justinian's masterpiece, Hagia Sophia, now a mosque.   Bruno Barbey/Magnum

The Empress Theodora and her court, from a mosaic in the Church of San Vitale, Ravenna, Italy. The Metropolitan Museum of Art, Fletcher Fund, 1925

untold. The finest structure, both architecturally and artistically, was Hagia Sophia (Church of the Holy Wisdom), built in the sixth century A.D. by the Emperor Justinian as the finest monument the Vicar of Christ could create on earth. Its dome, soaring 180 feet (55 meters) above the floor, seemed to believers to float unsupported in the air, like some magic carpet. (In reality the dome suspends from hidden buttresses.) When Justinian entered the building after its completion, he said, "Glory to God that I have been judged worthy of such a work. O Solomon, I have outdone you!"

Justinian's reputation rests in part on his contributions to the architectural beauty of Constantinople, as well as the reconquest, by his general Belisarius, of large parts of the former Roman Empire in the West, notably Italy and North Africa. But his major contribution was his code of laws, the Codex Justinianus. At one point in his reign, however, civil war threatened to overthrow and destroy the Byzantine capital. Battles broke out between the Greens and the Blues, groups that held opposing views as to the nature of Christ, and who had often come to blows over their beliefs. The two groups were also sporting clubs, sponsoring and wearing the colors of the chariot races which were a popular feature of Byzantine life. After one such "Sunday race" a riot broke out that turned quickly to civil war. Justinian found himself caught in the middle, in danger of losing not only his crown but also his head. They were both saved by his Queen, Theodora. The Emperor had tried to hide, but Theodora angrily pushed him to the front of the rioting crowd, shouting, "Make way! He who is born in the purple must be ready to die in the purple!" The spectacle of the Emperor taking command, robed in purple, calmed the crowd.

The Byzantine system had certain strengths that enabled it to survive for a thousand years against formidable enemies. Some Byzantine rulers were brilliant generals. Others were skilled at dividing the empire's adversaries through shrewd diplomacy. Militarily the Byzantine fleet controlled the Mediterranean; its most effective weapon was "Greek

Purple

Purple was the royal Byzantine color. It could be worn only by royalty. Justinian had set up a silk-weaving factory whose sole product was purple brocades. Empresses who were about to give birth were confined to a palace built of purple-speckled marble, so that their babies could be said to have been "born in the purple."

The Varangian Guard

One of the most important assets in the Byzantine military system was the Varangian Guard, foreign mercenaries recruited to be the emperor's personal bodyguard. Originally they were Vikings, chosen for their courage, martial skills, and physical appearance. It was a spectacular sight to see these tall blond warriors riding in full armor abreast of the Emperor as he rode through the streets en route to some public function or services at Hagia Sophia.

fire," a combustible mixture of boiling tar and pitch poured from huge pots onto attacking ships. Although Byzantine land armies were often outnumbered and poorly led, in emergencies the emperors could count on loyal nobles and the vast manpower reserves of Anatolia. They also made good use of foreign mercenaries, assuring their loyalty through high pay and special privileges.

Despite these strengths, the Byzantine system had serious weaknesses which limited its effectiveness. One major problem was the intrigue and corruption of the imperial court. The Byzantine system was to seclude imperial wives, female slaves, and concubines in the *gynacaeum,* a private area of the Emperor's palace (a custom later borrowed by the Ottoman Turks for the Sultan's harem), and much vicious infighting went on there over the succession as women vied for a ruler's favor to ensure the enthronement of their sons.

The empire's major weakness resulted from internal religious conflict. The ruling emperors insisted on the type of Christianity practiced by the Greek Orthodox Church. This insistence was made manifest in several ecumenical councils, the most important being the Council of Chalcedon (A.D. 451), which decided that Jesus Christ had two separate natures, one divine and the other human. Byzantine emperors ruthlessly

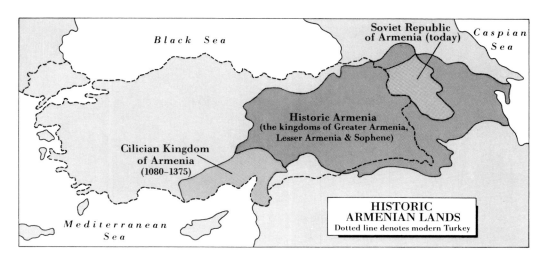

Map labels:
Black Sea
Soviet Republic of Armenia (today)
Caspian Sea
Historic Armenia (the kingdoms of Greater Armenia, Lesser Armenia & Sophene)
Cilician Kingdom of Armenia (1080–1375)
Mediterranean Sea

HISTORIC ARMENIAN LANDS
Dotted line denotes modern Turkey

persecuted all Christian groups that did not support the Orthodox position. The Armenians were the most severely persecuted, not only because they believed that human and divine were united in Jesus's nature, but also because Greater Armenia was near the Byzantine border with Persia, the major enemy. The Byzantines distrusted the Armenians' loyalty. Armenians under Byzantine control were heavily taxed, and thousands were deported to other parts of the empire. Ironically, several Byzantine emperors were Armenians, notably Leo "The Armenian" and John Tzimisces, one of the ablest generals ever to rule the empire.

When the Byzantines occupied all of Greater Armenia in the eleventh century A.D., large numbers of Armenians fleeing Byzantine persecution established a new Armenian kingdom in Cilicia on the Mediterranean coast. The Cilician Kingdom prospered for three centuries, playing an important role in Mediterranean trade due to its location. But hostility to the Byzantines elsewhere facilitated the expansion of the Turks, an invading nomadic people from central Asia. These Turks, relatively few in number but disciplined, skilled in warfare, stubborn, and patient, were destined to bring an end to a thousand years of rule in Anatolia by Christ's Vicars on Earth.

The Shadow of God

From this garden, like a moist bloom,
Blossomed those praiseworthy ones who
are the Ottoman House.

                 Mustafa Ali, *The Essence of History*

The first groups of Turks to arrive in Anatolia traveled in scattered, disciplined bands, rather like pioneer settlers of North America. As the historian Bernard Lewis notes, theirs was a frontier Islam; their teachers were wandering missionaries who preached "a militant faith, still full of the pristine fire and directness of the first Muslims, a religion of warriors, whose creed was a battle cry, a call to arms." Turkish warriors who did great deeds in the service of Islam were rewarded with lands and often the title of Gazi, "hero of the faith," by the caliphs and local rulers whom they served.

One such Gazi, Seljuk, was the leader of a Turkish group that settled in eastern Anatolia, near the border of the Byzantine Empire, after moving west from northern Iran.

In 1071 a Seljuk force routed a much larger Byzantine army near Manzikert (modern Malazgirt) in eastern Anatolia, capturing the Emperor in the process. He was eventually ransomed, but the defeat opened

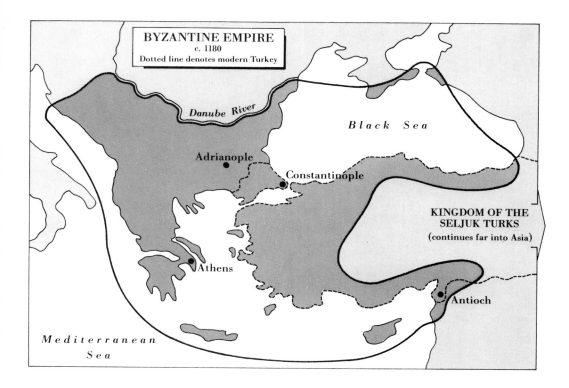

the way for other Turkish peoples to migrate into the peninsula. Byzantine power was reduced to a few fortified cities such as Trabzon. The Seljuks controlled much of Anatolia, but other Turkish dynasties challenged them. As a result there was no central government as competing Islamic and Christian rulers fought for power.

The Seljuks never succeeded in controlling Anatolia. They seem to have remained nomads at heart, capable of bursts of military and creative energy, but not of efficient administration of conquered territories. Yet their political failure was more than matched by great artistic and cultural achievements. At a time of disaster for Islam, when Mongol hordes swept over the Caliph's lands, a brief but extraordinary flowering of Islamic civilization took place in the Seljuk Sultanate of Rum in remote central Anatolia.

The Sultanate of Rum

This "golden age" of Seljuk-inspired Islamic culture centered in the city of Konya, capital of the Seljuk Sultanate of Rum—so called because the Seljuks had occupied territories of the Byzantine Empire; *Rum* is the Islamic name for Rome. Protected by its walls, its horse archers and cavalry, and a chain of fortresslike hostelries called *hans* (inns) or caravanserais for travelers located strategically a day's ride apart along the old Roman roads, the sultanate devoted itself to peaceful pursuits. Philosophers, poets, potters, craftsmen, and refugees from Mongol invasions flocked to the Seljuk court. One of the most influential arrivals was Celaleddin Rumi, better known as Mevlana ("Our Lord"), a distinguished Islamic scholar and founder of the order of the Mevlevi ("Whirling") Dervishes. There were many such orders in Islam (the word dervish comes from a Persian word meaning "poor") devoted to lives of meditation and worship. Each order had its particular form of worship. The Whirling Dervishes emphasized the ritual of dance designed to bring them through endless repetitions of whirling, to unity with God. They wore long, white, full-skirted robes and tall conical red hats when they danced, spinning ever faster to the music of the flute, violin, and drum until they reached a state of trance. Mevlana taught that man is not only God's creation, but also his reflection. Only love is important. Reason keeps man apart from God. Man is physically parted from God, but he longs to return. Music and the stately ritual of the dance help men free themselves from the bondage of this earth and abandon themselves to God's love.

In the thirteenth century one group of migrating Turks settled on the

Loading cargo at Trabzon, an important port and ancient fortress on the Black Sea.
Turkish Tourism Office

A group of Whirling Dervishes perform for the crowd. Banned in the early years of the republic because Atatürk felt they were obstacles to social progress, they now perform their ritual dance at Konya annually in the great hall where Mevlana's disciples once danced, as a kind of link for modern Turks with their rich Seljuk past. Turkish Tourism Office

fringes of Seljuk territory near the Byzantine border. Little is known of their origins, but apparently they rendered important services to Seljuk rulers in their struggles with the Christians and received grants of land in return. The Turks belonging to this particular group called themselves *Osmanlis*, "sons of Osman," after their leader, Osman, in accordance with ancient Turkish tradition. The name, corrupted into English as "Ottomans," has come down in history to denote the warriors who not only established Islamic control over all of Anatolia but also founded an empire that eventually spanned three continents.

With Ottoman success the term "Turk" fell into disrepute; it was used only to refer to a country bumpkin or illiterate peasant. The English traveler W. M. Ramsay observed in 1897 that this was still the case: "One would mutter 'Turk kafa' whereas in English we would say 'Blockhead!'"

Profiting from Byzantine weakness and rivalry among the various Muslim rulers of Anatolia, Osman and his successors expanded their territories rapidly. In 1326 they captured the important Byzantine city of Bursa. Orhan (Orkhan), Osman's eldest son and successor, made it the first permanent Ottoman capital.

By the late 1300's Ottoman armies had crossed the Straits into Europe, capturing all of Thrace from the Byzantines. The major city of the province, Adrianople, renamed Edirne, became the second Ottoman capital. Constantinople was now completely encircled by Ottoman power, although its fleet still provided access to the outside world.

Sultans

Orhan was also the first Ottoman leader to assume the title of Sultan. This title, which appears in the Koran, is used there to denote authority in the general sense of the word. The Islamic caliphs granted it as a title of honor for rulers who controlled territory, but continued to acknowledge the caliphs as their spiritual overlords. Seljuk rulers later upgraded the title to emphasize their role as military and political leaders in fairly well-defined territories. After the line of caliphs came to an end, it became the standard designation for rulers who held power and recognized no superior save Allah.

Mehmet the Conqueror

After several abortive attempts the Ottomans, on May 29, 1453, captured the great city of Constantinople. It was a feat that no other non-Christian besieger had been able to achieve.

Constantinople had been "captured" in 1204 by Christian Crusaders allied with one of the Byzantine factions competing for power. It was sacked and burned by its so-called allies, and ruled by usurpers until 1261, when Michael VIII Palaeologus, who had continued the legitimate Byzantine imperial line in exile, recaptured the city.

The capture of the Byzantine capital was primarily due to Sultan Mehmet II, who added the epithet Fatih (Conqueror) to his name after the conquest. Mehmet Fatih succeeded for a number of reasons. For one, he was fortunate in the political situation of the time. The Pope, Nicholas V, resented the Byzantine Emperor's claim to equality with him as spiritual lord of Christendom, and discouraged European rulers from sending the emperor any aid. These rulers obeyed the Pope, and other than a company of mercenaries from the independent Italian city of Genoa, no Christian volunteers came to join the emperor's depleted forces in Constantinople.

But Mehmet's military strategy and tactics had a great deal more to do with the conquest than politics. The Byzantine fleet was not only strong; it was also protected by a huge boom stretched across the entrance to the Golden Horn so that it could not be surprised at anchor. Mehmet ordered his construction engineers to build a logging road of greased timbers, set in a frame so they would roll on pins. The special pathway began at a landing point hidden from the view of Byzantine sentinels. The Ottoman fleet was hauled up this inclined road on pulleys, ship by ship, overland and downhill to the water's edge, where they were refloated behind the Byzantine fleet. With their sails hoisted, flags flying, and oars waving in the air, it must have seemed to the astonished Byzantines, whose view of the logging road was blocked by the high ground, that the Ottomans were possessed of some miraculous power.

Constantinople held out for seven bloody weeks. Then on May 29, as the Ottomans made an all-out assault, the Genoese commander received a mortal wound, and by mistake a small side gate in the walls was left unbolted. As the attackers poured through, the last Byzantine emperor, ironically named Constantine XII, tore off the imperial double-eagle insignia from his armor and, shouting, "All is lost. Save yourselves," plunged into the battle, never to be seen again.

And thus it was that after a thousand years, the city of God, no longer bedecked like a young bride with gold and jewels but old, exhausted, penniless, passed into Muslim hands.

The Grandeur of Empire

The conquest of Constantinople made the Ottomans a world power of the first rank. Mehmet II was saluted as *Fatih*, and in subsequent years he added the last remaining Byzantine territories in Anatolia to his empire. The Conqueror's successors, notably Selim I and Süleyman I, expanded the empire to include southern Russia and the Balkans in Europe; Egypt, Algeria, Tunisia, and Libya in North Africa; and the eastern lands of the caliphs as far as Iran. The empire reached its greatest extent in the reign of Süleyman (1520–1566).

The almost continuous Ottoman military success created an aura of invincibility for them. Their victories on land were matched by those at sea. Almost the only reverses suffered by the Ottoman fleet were the

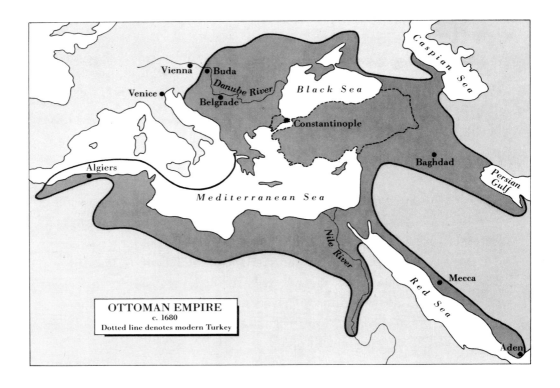

OTTOMAN EMPIRE
c. 1680
Dotted line denotes modern Turkey

unsuccessful siege of the island of Malta, then ruled by the warrior Knights of Malta, and defeat at the hands of a Christian navy at the battle of Lepanto (1571). Otherwise, control of the Mediterranean remained in the hands of the Ottomans and their auxiliaries, the corsair navies of Algiers, Tunis, and Tripoli.

Success led to a sense of superiority over Christian rulers as the sultans became arrogant. Correspondence from European rulers to them always began with a list of titles. The Sultan was addressed as Defender of the Faith, Lord of the Age, Sovereign of the Two Seas, Guardian of the Holy Places (Mecca and Medina), for example. The sultans would reply in kind; Sultan Murad III once replied to a communication from Queen Elizabeth I of England as follows: "Your letter has reached Our Splendid Threshold, the Orbit of Felicity and the Lofty Lintel of Justice."

The title above all others that underlined the power of the sultans was "Shadow of God." The title defined the Sultan's position, in effect, as that of the direct representative of God on earth, holding the highest position in the divine arrangement of the world. In political terms he *was* the state, as shown in the Turkish saying *"Devlet baba, memleket cocukları"* ("The state is father, the people are children"). The Shadow of God role was symbolized by the ceremonial parasol held above the Sultan's head by a bearer to shield him from the merciless Middle Eastern sun during his public appearances.

Slaves of the Sultan

The core of the sultan's army was a special unit called the Janissaries. "Janissary" is an English corruption of the Turkish *yeni çeri*, "new troops." Under Islamic custom one fifth of all booty captured in wars against the enemies of the faith was reserved for the ruler under whom a victorious Muslim army served. Ottoman sultans used the privilege to choose the bravest and strongest prisoners of war for their personal guard. Originally they were prisoners of war, but as the Ottomans expanded their territory, they set up a conscription system to ensure a steady supply of manpower. A recruiting team would visit a village and pick out the best physical specimens from among the boys up to the age of twelve. The recruits were Christian, on the theory that a freeborn Muslim could not become a "slave" to the Sultan. They were brought to Constantinople and formally converted to Islam in a simple ceremony, and from then on they became the ruler's property.

The Christian population, although it had little choice, often attempted to avoid the losses of manpower needed in their villages through such methods as child marriage and hiding their most promising boys prior to the arrival of the recruiting teams, and religious leaders would protest to Ottoman officials when the drain on a particular village or region became too great. But despite the separation from their homes and families and the often arbitrary nature of the conscription process, there were compensations for the recruits. They were paid regularly and well, housed in their own quarters in Topkapı Palace (the official residence of the sultans), and collectively held a privileged position in the Ottoman government. Few Janissaries ever voluntarily left the service, and although later on they became corrupted by easy living and privileged status, during much of the period of the empire the rigorous discipline produced an esprit de corps not unlike that of the U.S. Marine Corps. And in terms of being near the center of Ottoman power, these converts to Islam had a great advantage over most freeborn Muslim Turks.

The Ottoman Ruling System

Ottoman administration was a model of decentralization, economy of management, and efficiency for its time. The administrative system was centered on the Sultan, whose power was absolute. The only check on his power came from his obligation to obey and uphold the sacred law of Islam.

The Sultan also had the right to issue edicts having the force of law, as long as they did not conflict with Islamic law. Süleyman I's greatest contribution to the empire was not his military victories but his code of laws. For this reason he is known as Süleyman Kanuni, "Lawgiver." His laws *(kanunlar)* set high standards for justice and eliminated many abuses, assuring equal treatment for his Muslim subjects under the law of Islam. The religious leaders *(ulema)* whose job it was to interpret Islamic law were required to make sure that edicts and decisions by the sultans conformed to the law. If they believed that an edict or decision was contrary to Islamic law, they would issue a binding legal opinion *(fetva)* to that effect. But this did not happen very often. It was to the advantage of both ruler and religious leaders to cooperate.

Here are some examples of kanunlar: a system of fines was installed to replace Islamic corporal punishment for many crimes, mistreatment of animals became a punishable offense, arbitrary land confiscation was prohibited by one *kanun*, and another reduced the poll tax for Christian subjects. Süleyman's code was highly regarded well beyond the borders of the empire; Christian families from nearby countries such as Hungary often took refuge in Ottoman territory to escape arbitrary taxes imposed upon them by their own rulers.

To run their empire efficiently, the Ottomans developed an unusual method of dealing with non-Muslim conquered peoples based on ethnic and religious affiliation. Peoples who had their own ethnic and cultural bonds and sacred scriptures (Bible or Torah, for example) were dealt with as *millets*, a Turkish word loosely translated as "nations." They could practice their religions freely and were allowed to manage their internal community affairs under their own elected or appointed leaders. Jews, Greek Orthodox Christians, and Armenians formed the three major *millets*. Members of a *millet* were required to swear obedience to the Sultan, to pay a poll tax, and to accept second-class status; there were also strict laws on how they could dress, act in public, or build their homes. For example, no Christian house could be taller than a Muslim one, and the ringing of church bells for services was prohibited since it would annoy their Muslim neighbors "sleeping in" on Sundays.

But in return the *millets* received certain protections. Although prohibited from bearing arms, they were generally protected by the Ottoman military and not interfered with in the conduct of their personal lives or practice of their religion. The head of each *millet*, rabbi, patriarch, or priest, served as its representative before the sultan.

The Ottoman government also developed a method of dealing with foreign rulers in matters of trade that worked effectively for a long time, contributing to the empire's economic growth. This method is referred

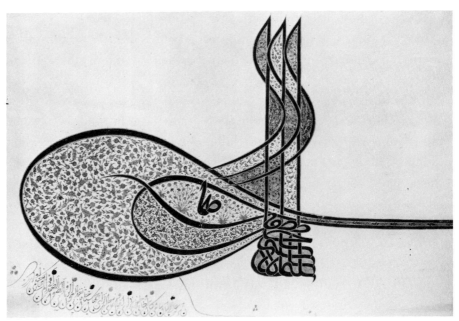

Tuğra of Süleyman the Magnificent, from an imperial edict. The Metropolitan Museum of Art, Rogers Fund, 1938

to as the Capitulations. "To capitulate" usually means "to surrender," but when used correctly it refers to the chapters (*capitula* in Latin) of a treaty agreement or contract. The Capitulations extended what we would today call diplomatic immunity, or extraterritorial privileges, to citizens of European countries residing or working in Ottoman cities; by extension it included non-Muslim subjects of the empire employed by European merchants or consuls. They were exempt from Ottoman taxes; more important, they were not subject to Ottoman law, only to the laws and taxes of their own country. Ottoman officials and even police could enter their homes and businesses only by invitation, and

Selimiye Mosque, Edirne, considered by many to be architect Sinan's masterpiece. Turkish Tourism Office

goods stored in the warehouses of European merchants could not be confiscated even if a merchant owed money to an Ottoman citizen.

The first treaty of Capitulations was signed with Venice in 1521. It was followed by similar ones with France, England, Holland, and other European trading nations. As long as the empire remained strong and its European rivals weak and divided, it was an effective means of assuring a prosperous trade. Each capitulatory treaty began with the phrase: "Graciously accorded by the Sultan, ever victorious, to the infidel King of _____, ever vanquished." The Sultan would seal the bargain with his *tuğra*, the imperial monogram. Each *tuğra* was designed exclusively for a reigning Sultan and left office with him. It bore his name, with a list of titles and verses from the Koran in elaborate calligraphy.

Life at the Ottoman court was quite sophisticated. Sultans such as Mehmet Fatih, feared for their military skill by European rulers, were

also patrons of the arts, science, literature, and especially architecture. Mehmet maintained good relations with a number of European kings and sent emissaries to their courts from time to time. In 1479 he sent an invitation to the Venetian court painter Gentile Bellini to come to Constantinople to paint his portrait. The result was the famous Bellini portrait showing a ruler in repose, his bearded face unlined, wearing a white turban and a wool mantle draped over his shoulders. (It hangs in the National Gallery in London.) The portrait befits a man accustomed to command, but one who also wrote poetry, patronized artists and writers with large gifts of money, and liked to spend long hours in the company of scholars and philosophers, with whom he debated important philosophical questions.

Ottoman Influences on Modern Turkey

The six centuries of rule by a single Ottoman dynasty set its stamp on modern Turkey in a number of areas. In architecture the work of Mimar Sinan, Chief Court Architect to Süleyman I, not only resulted in the skyline of Istanbul and the mosques and other buildings of many Ottoman cities, but established a distinctive Ottoman style of architecture. Originally a Christian youth recruited into the Janissaries and trained as a civil engineer, Sinan made lasting contributions to Ottoman Islamic culture during his long and productive life. He served in the post for fifty years and designed some 360 structures, the finest being the Selimiye Mosque in Edirne and the Süleymaniye Mosque in Istanbul. The year 1988, the four hundredth anniversary of his death, was officially named Architect Sinan Year in his honor.

The thread of modern social life in Turkey also draws upon Ottoman models and has preserved a number of elements from its predecessor. The Turkish national folktale teller, Nasreddin Hoca, lived in Ottoman

Friday prayers in the Süleymaniye Mosque.   Sharon Guynup

Camel wrestling, still a popular sport in southeastern Turkey.   Turkish Tourism Office

times, developing his satiric humor in comic situations recorded in countless tales. Hoca is considered so funny by Turks that the mere mention of his name sets people laughing. The shadow puppet plays, *karagöz*, also have been a part of Turkish life at all levels, village and urban alike, and although the genre originated elsewhere, the Ottoman version draws upon fourteenth-century individuals. Similarly, such popular entertainment sports as greased wrestling and camel wrestling, the Turkish love of flowers, the proverbs and folktales preserved in oral literature, Islamic festivals and holidays, all help to link the people with their past.

Preparing for a "greased wrestling" contest.   Turkish Tourism Office

Decline and Fall

If God closes one door, He opens a thousand others.

Turkish proverb

The decline and fall of the Ottoman Empire was a long slow process. As was the case with Rome, internal institutions of government weakened and decayed before territories were overrun by enemies. The failure of the Ottomans to develop an effective procedure for the succession to the throne proved to be a major weakness in later years. The only eligibility requirement was that the ruling Sultan be a male descendant of Osman; members of the family could not agree to any other arrangement. In the early stages of the empire the succession did pass from eldest son to eldest son, and the fact that these sons were men of ability helped make the system work. But the expansion of the Sultan's harem, with up to four legitimate wives and many mistresses competing to promote their sons' chances, created much conflict. The death of a ruling Sultan invariably set off a power struggle lasting until one prince had outmaneuvered all the others. Then he would kill all his rivals, at least those he could reach, to ensure his accession.

In the mid-seventeenth century, due to this fratricidal practice, the House of Osman almost ran out of males on a couple of occasions. As a result an arrangement called the *kafes* ("cage") was introduced. When a Sultan died, all his sons except the one designated to succeed him were locked away in separate suites of rooms in Topkapı Palace. They remained in their suites for the rest of their lives, guarded day and night by gigantic eunuchs. Sometimes a prince who had been locked up in this fashion succeeded to the throne, either by chance or because there were no other candidates. By that time, if he had not gone mad, he was totally inexperienced in the ways of the outside world and unfit to govern an empire.

End of the Janissaries

The deterioration in discipline and effectiveness of the Janissaries also undermined the ruling system. The Janissary units in Constantinople became a serious problem for the sultans from the seventeenth century onward. Their barracks in the Topkapı Palace complex, literally under the ruler's nose, made it both simple and effective for them to display their displeasure at the food or pay. If they were unhappy with either or both, they would overturn the kettles that held their rations and the corps' drummers would bang loudly on their drums as a warning to the Sultan. It was a rare Sultan who did not accede to Janissary demands; one ruler, Osman II, was deposed and murdered by them, and others came near to losing their thrones to these kingmakers.

For all practical purposes the Sultan had become the slave of his guardsmen by the early 1800's. By then the Janissaries were of little value in the defense of the empire. Their equipment was outdated, and they refused to learn new tactics from European instructors hired to train the Ottoman armies. Finally in 1826 the ruling Sultan, Mahmud

II, figured out a way to get rid of them. He formed a special army, trained by European advisers and equipped with cannon. He then held up the Janissaries' pay to provoke a riot, surrounded their barracks with his special army, and blew them all up.

The *millet* system and the Capitulations also turned into liabilities for the Ottomans. By the nineteenth century people's ideas about freedom had progressed. European military superiority over the Ottomans led to increased pressures on the Sultan to allow greater freedom for the non-Muslim population, encouraging subject peoples to assert their independence. Aided by a general breakdown in Ottoman authority in the European provinces, Greeks, Serbians, Albanians, and others broke free from Ottoman control. The Armenians, perhaps due to their heavy involvement in the empire's business affairs, remained loyal.

Misuse of the Capitulations hurt the empire's economy. Because of their limited knowledge of the outside world and their lack of familiarity with foreign languages, Ottoman officials found it easier to depend on non-Muslim agents in matters of trade. As a result certain Greeks, Armenians, and Jews became indispensable to the Ottoman government as interpreters, translators, and go-betweens in trade or treaty negotiations. They helped arrange loans from European banks to bail out the Ottoman treasury when it was faced with financial ruin due to disastrous wars. As a result of these services a number of non-Muslim merchants, bankers, and traders became wealthy, arousing envy on the part of Ottoman officials. Envy in time turned to hate, leading indirectly to brutal repression of minorities in the time of Sultan Abdul Hamid II (1876–1909).

The *Tanzimat* Reforms

In the nineteenth century a few farsighted sultans and intellectual leaders tried to introduce reforms into the ruling system. They believed

The castle built by Ishak Pasha in the 1800's stands in the rough country outside of the town of Doğubeyazit, near Mount Ararat. Joseph Lawton

they could reform the system from the top downward, using ideas and institutions borrowed directly from Europe. The first reforming Sultan, Selim III, tried to form a European-style army trained by European instructors, equipped with the new European weapons developed in the Napoleonic wars, and outfitted in uniforms borrowed from various European countries. However, when the Janissaries got wind of the project, they overturned their cooking pots in rebellion. They felt that the "New Army" constituted a threat to their privileged position within the Ottoman system, and forced Selim to abdicate.

Selim's successors, Mahmud II and Abdul Mecid, were more prudent and fortunate. With the Janissaries out of the way, they issued decrees in 1839 and 1861 that have come to be known as *Tanzimat*, meaning

Dolmabahçe *("Stuffed Garden"), a palace built by Sultan Abdul Mecid in the nineteenth century in a European style, imitating the home of the French kings at Versailles.*
Ankara Archaeological Museum

literally "Reordering." The decrees were issued partly in response to European criticism that the sultans had no interest in improving the lives of their subjects. But their main purpose was to enable the rulers to strengthen the power of the government while appearing to encourage the establishment of social services and institutions similar to those in Europe. One of the first institutions established under the decrees was a school system that offered such subjects as physics, chemistry, mathematics, history, geography, and foreign languages in the curriculum.

Other decrees established a medical school, a military academy staffed by European advisers, and a law school. The question of law was particularly troublesome to the reformers, because the empire was governed under Islamic law, which they believed proceeded directly from God to man in the Koran. In both theory and practice only the religious leaders could interpret the law, and they were strongly opposed to changes that might weaken their hold over the people or limit their power.

Although the *Tanzimat* reformers were serious men, committed to endowing the empire with institutions that would refute its critics, they did not contemplate any basic changes in the ruling system. This fact, plus the opposition of religious leaders, limited their effectiveness. In any case the reforms had little effect on the lives of the general population. Muslim and non-Muslim villages alike suffered from crushing taxation, exploitation by large landowners and moneylenders, and in the case of non-Muslims periodic attacks by Kurdish bandits, angry mobs, or even the soldiery of the empire.

A Tanzimat *decree fixed agricultural taxes at 10 percent, but a tax collector who came to a village was as likely as not to demand 15 or 20 percent, usually in cash. To raise this money tenants and small farmers were forced to turn to moneylenders, who charged anywhere from 20 to 120 percent interest.*

The Sick Man of Europe

By the latter part of the nineteenth century European rulers had become convinced that the empire should be destroyed. Conditions had become so unstable that the sultanate was referred to as "the Sick Man of Europe," as if land and ruler were suffering from the same illness.

A fitful hope that the empire might recover gleamed in 1876 when a new Sultan, Abdul Hamid II, came to the throne. Representatives of

the European powers as well as his own advisers strongly urged him to introduce reforms. If he did not, they said, the empire would fall apart. These advisers knew that leaders could provide basic rights for their people and still remain in power. The best way to accomplish this was by a constitution.

Abdul Hamid reluctantly agreed to issue a constitution. This document established the empire's first parliament, the Grand National Assembly. Most of its members were appointed; they were either government officials, religious leaders, or intellectuals. The mass of the people had no more say in national affairs than in the past, but the fact that an absolute ruler had issued a written document limiting his power was a major break with the Ottoman past.

However, Abdul Hamid was not one to be deterred by a piece of paper. Less than a year after he had approved the constitution, he suspended it, under his constitutional power as final arbiter in the system. He also disbanded the Assembly, saying that the deputies were interested only in criticizing him and not in developing responsible legislation. There was some truth to the Sultan's charges, especially as the deputies had no understanding of the democratic process in lawmaking. But Abdul Hamid's main goal was to rule like the Shadow of God of old. For the next thirty years he did just that.

During that period it seemed as if the clock had been turned back to an earlier Ottoman century. The Sultan trusted no one; he had an elaborate system of spies and hired spies to spy on the spies. His food had to be tasted by three people before he would eat it. He slept with a loaded gun under his pillow. Books were censored, telephones were tapped regularly, and Christians were not allowed to travel without a permit.

Abdul Hamid II (1842–1918), last Shadow of God on earth.   The Bettmann Archive

The darkest chapter in Abdul Hamid's grim era was undoubtedly the massacres of Armenians carried out in 1895–96. An estimated 300,000 Armenians died in these massacres, which seemed to have developed from a morbid fear in Abdul Hamid's mind that the supposedly "loyal *millet*" was actually conspiring with European powers to overthrow him. The organization of underground Armenian revolutionary groups to defend villagers against attacks by Kurdish bandits and irregular Ottoman soldiers helped to bring on the massacres, as the entire Armenian population was blamed for anti-government violence. The repression finally was stopped after the European powers warned they would intervene. But the massacres left a legacy of hatred between Armenian and Turk that led to even worse atrocities in World War I and has lasted up to the present day.

In order to improve the Ottoman army, Abdul Hamid hired European advisers and sent promising young officers to Europe for advanced training. These young officers observed firsthand the great advances in industrialization in Europe. They began to compare the empire unfavorably with Europe. Increasingly, it seemed to them that the Sultan was responsible for its backwardness. Some of them planned secretly to overthrow Abdul Hamid and restore constitutional government.

In 1908 a committee of officers decided to act. The deteriorating international situation seemed to indicate that the European rulers were finally about to unite to bury the Sick Man. A meeting of the King of England and the Czar of Russia suggested that the empire could no longer rely on British support against the ancient Russian enemy. The young officers raised the flag of revolt, demanding that the Sultan reinstate the constitution. When nearly all the army backed their demands, Abdul Hamid capitulated. A year later he was packed off into exile. His brother, Mehmet Reshad, was released from the cage where had had spent thirty years of his life and escorted down the Bosporus to the palace to receive the traditional hundred-and-one-gun salute as

Downtown Pera, the European quarter of Constantinople (now called Istanbul) early in the twentieth century.   The Bettmann Archive

Mehmet V. It is said that he turned white with fear and fainted when the first cannon was fired.

The Military Takes Control

For a brief time after the removal of Abdul Hamid the empire's peoples were united. Christians, Jews, and Muslims shook hands, danced in the streets, talked excitedly of a new order. But this new order was not to be; God had opened one door and then abruptly closed it. A new Sultan held the throne, but real power was in the hands of a revolutionary group, the Committee for Union and Progress. Within this group three leaders ruled as a dictatorial triumvirate, and once again constitutional government became a sham, as these leaders governed to suit themselves. Their main goals were to restore Ottoman military strength in relation to Europe and rebuild Ottoman (i.e. Turkish) nationalism as the guiding spirit of the empire. The three leaders were not interested in promoting the welfare of the non-Muslim population—or for that matter in improving the lives of their fellow Turks. Instead they talked vaguely of pan-Turkism, a movement that would unite all Turkish-speaking peoples in a great empire.

The most powerful figure in the triumvirate, Enver Pasha, had served in Germany as military attaché in Berlin and admired German efficiency, organization, and technical skills. After the Balkan Wars of 1912–1913, which resulted in defeat and more losses of territory in eastern Europe, Enver decided to align the empire with Germany. He felt that England and France had instigated their Balkan allies to start

Ottoman Mehmets *(soldiers) marching through the streets of Constantinople (Istanbul) at the start of the First World War.*   AP/Wide World Photo

the war as a means of undermining the empire. Germany, on the other hand, seemed to have no designs whatsoever on Ottoman territory.

As the threat of world war loomed, Enver decided that the empire should join Germany in a common front against England, France, and czarist Russia. He abandoned the long-standing policy of the sultans of playing European powers against each other to ensure the empire's survival, and signed a secret alliance with the German government. It was to prove to be a fatal mistake.

The terms of the alliance stipulated that in the event of war, the Ottomans would act to neutralize the Russian fleet in the Black Sea, close the Straits, and tie up Russian armies in the east so that Germany would not have to fight on two fronts. Two German battle cruisers were brought secretly to Constantinople. When World War I broke out in September 1914, the cruisers, renamed and flying the Ottoman flag, steamed north into the Black Sea and bombarded Russian naval installations, sinking many ships in harbor. Russia reacted with a land invasion through the Caucasus Mountains, the traditional route for invaders from the east. Although a combined Anglo-Australian-New Zealand expeditionary force failed to capture the Straits, the British naval blockade in the Mediterranean and British success in organizing an "Arab Revolt" in the eastern provinces had the desired effect for the empire's enemies. Enver's pro-German policy had rebounded with disastrous results; the empire was now surrounded by hostile forces.

The war years were harrowing ones for the people of the empire. They were particularly hard on the ordinary soldiers, the Mehmets, about whom the poet Nazim Hikmet was to write later in moving terms:

Mehmets, poor Mehmets
And the years of the Great War, and the faces of Mehmets
Wrenched out of the darkness
And torn to shreds on the black brambles.

"Written in Blood"

Another tragic chapter in the long history of the Armenians was "written in blood" during the war, when the majority of this population was forcibly deported from eastern Anatolia in 1915–16. Large-scale deportation and slaughter of particular peoples has occurred often in past history in many areas, as rulers or leaders have sought to purge their lands of potentially disloyal or ethnically different groups. But the Armenians are a special case, due not only to the numbers involved but also to the controversy surrounding their deportation. We know that some Armenian revolutionary organizations were sympathetic to the invading Russians, and still more were *accused* of collaborating with the enemy. These nationalists declared that their goal was to establish an independent Armenian state after the war. But the Ottoman government undertook to remove the *entire* Armenian population from eastern Anatolia, supposedly as a protective measure but also to rid themselves of potential internal opposition. The removal was carried out by irregular troops with Kurdish militiamen as guards. The Armenians were to be resettled away from the eastern war zone, in areas still under Ottoman control in Lebanon, Syria, and Palestine. The deportations were marked by great brutality on the part of the guards, perhaps in the desire to settle scores with Christian villagers, but the Armenians also suffered from the hardships of the march and from starvation, heat, and thirst.

There is also no agreement on the number of Armenians deported or the number of casualties; the death toll estimates ranged from 300,000 to two million. What is clear is that a large noncombatant civilian population suffered untold horrors as a result of war and wartime policy decisions. The collapse of the Ottoman government after World War I prevented any immediate investigation. Since then successive Turkish governments have consistently dissociated themselves from the policies of their Ottoman predecessors. They take the position that they cannot be held accountable for actions they took no part in and would not have approved of in any case.

During the first half century of the republic the "Armenian question" was not a factor in Turkish foreign or domestic policies. But in the 1970's the issue was revived by a new generation of Armenians seeking to bring the Turks before the bar of international judgment. Since there are no Armenians left in Turkey other than a small unobtrusive minority in Istanbul, the issue affects the country only in its relations with other countries where there are large Armenian populations, such as the United States. But there are important moral and ethical implications that may be examined in questions such as the following:

1. Are there analogies (or similarities) between the Ottoman treatment of the Armenians and the U.S. government's treatment of Native American Indian tribes or the Nazis' murder of the Jews?
2. Should governments be held accountable at all times for actions of their predecessors?
3. If you had been Enver Pasha, given the conditions of war at the time (impending defeat, public hysteria, difficult field communications, a desire to eliminate minorities, etc.), how would you have proceeded with regard to the Armenians?
4. Do military commanders in war have an obligation to respect the basic rights of a surrounding civilian population even if they believe that population is likely to be hostile?
5. Do ends ever justify means?

Yet these ordinary soldiers held off the armies of England and Russia, while their German allies were preoccupied with trench warfare in Europe and gave them little help. The Mehmets had antiquated rifles and bayonets; their enemies had modern artillery, tanks, automatic weapons, even airplanes. The Mehmets' uniforms, baggy cotton pants and thin shirts, provided little protection in the snows of eastern Anatolia. Enver had not planned on a long winter campaign, and as many soldiers died from the weather as from Russian guns.

The civilian population also suffered. Past wars between Ottoman and European armies had been fought outside Anatolia, but in this one the peninsula became a battleground. Muslim and non-Muslim villages alike were destroyed as the tide of battle shifted between Turks and invading Russians.

The End of Empire

In October 1918, before the Germans agreed to an armistice, the Ottoman government signed such an agreement with England and France. British warships steamed up the Straits, and British and French troops mounted guard over the Sultan's palace. A French general rode into the Ottoman capital on a white horse in imitation of Mehmet Fatih's triumphal entry nearly five centuries earlier. While the victorious Allies argued over how to divide up the empire's last remaining territories and thus complete the burial of the Sick Man, the surviving Mehmets either wandered home to their Anatolian villages in rags, despairing and leaderless, or took to the hills as outlaws.

Out of the Ashes— Atatürk's Revolution

The foe thrusts his knife into the heart of the land,
There was none to save our ill-fated mother.

Namik Kemal

Constantinople, in the grim winter of 1918, was a defeated city, capital of a defeated empire. The city's residents went about their business listlessly with a sense of imminent doom. Nothing worked; there was no coal and little wood for heat, and the ferryboats on which people depended for transportation across the Bosporus ran infrequently for lack of fuel. The crime rate rose drastically as law and order became almost nonexistent; few policemen were to be seen, and almost the only protection was that provided by small detachments of Allied occupation soldiers. Citizens barricaded themselves in their homes at night, emerging in the daylight hours as furtive shadows to buy bread and other necessities—if these could even be had—at inflated prices. Ottoman currency was so devalued as to be worthless; it took a day's wages to buy a loaf of round gray Turkish bread. It seemed almost a disgrace to be a Turk in this once-proud capital. Some people shed their fezzes and pretended to be Europeans in order to obtain jobs with the occupation authorities.

The Shadow of God still sat on his throne, but the European powers were meeting in Paris to pronounce last rites for the Sick Man, dividing Ottoman territories among themselves in accordance with secret wartime agreements. In addition to the former Arab provinces of Syria, Lebanon, and Palestine, Anatolia became part of the spoils of war.

Greece had fought an earlier war with the Turks in 1913, and England and France had promised the country some territory in Anatolia in a secret agreement. The dream of one day restoring a Byzantine empire in the east had never died in Greek hearts, and to Greek leaders the time seemed ripe. Encouraged by promises of British support, the Greek army landed at Smyrna (now Izmir) in May 1919, and began moving inland along the broad river valleys of the Aegean coastal area.

The Greek invasion was a final blow to Turkish pride. Outlaw bands of Mehmets began harassing the advancing Greek forces. But their efforts were like pinpricks in the hide of an elephant. The Ottoman government could offer no support; the wartime leaders had fled the country, and the Sultan could only wring his hands and "weep like a woman," as he told an aide. An angry crowd gathered outside the Blue

Halide Edib

The woman in black was Halide Edib, daughter of an Ottoman aristocrat and the first female graduate of Robert College. She went on to become a journalist and public figure at a time when most Turkish women stayed at home. Halide Edib became a close associate of Mustafa Kemal; her memoirs and reports on the war for independence are an invaluable reference for the period.

Mosque in Constantinople, waving black flags and shouting for action. Unexpectedly, an unveiled woman in black pushed through the crowd, mounted a speaker's stand, and cried: "Brothers, sisters, countrymen, when the night is blackest and seems eternal, the light of dawn is nearest." Not only her words but her very appearance were prophetic of a new age dawning for the Turkish nation, an age when Turkish women would walk unveiled in public and work alongside men, and Turks would stand tall and proud behind a new national hero.

A New Leader Emerges

A Turkish proverb says "Destiny caresses the few and molests the many." In this darkest hour for the Turkish people, an inspired leader came before them as if to fulfill the proverb. It was his destiny not only to restore Turkish dignity and pride after these qualities had been largely lost, but also to lead Turkey into the twentieth-century world of secular nations.

As a child the leader was known simply as Mustafa. The name was a common one in Muslim families, but this Mustafa was marked for special things early in life; he was a forthright child with a keen intelligence and penetrating blue eyes who was always asking questions. His father, who had been a soldier in the Sultan's army, wanted Mustafa to follow a military career; his mother, daughter of a prosperous land-owner and somewhat better educated than her husband, hoped that Mustafa would grow up to become an Islamic teacher *(hoca)* or scholar. There was much debate between them over this issue. But he had problems at the Koranic school that he first attended in deference to his mother's wishes. His father then enrolled him in a different school, one with a European-style curriculum, established in the late nineteenth century as a result of the *Tanzimat* reforms. In this school Mustafa stood out as the brightest among the students. At his father's untimely death, however, his mother reentered him in the Koranic school, where he continued to struggle and eventually dropped out.

Fortunately for Turkey and its future, Mustafa kept his father's dream in mind, and one day, encouraged by a neighbor who was a retired military officer, he took the entrance examinations for the nearby military secondary school. He passed with flying colors, and at last his mother relented. Thus in different ways each parent contributed to his career, his father by encouraging his military interests, and his mother by insisting that he persevere in his education. His mother lived into her nineties to see her son become a teacher in the true sense of the word, guiding his people into the modern world and tutoring them toward understanding and acceptance of new ways.

Mustafa did so well in his studies that one of his teachers, Captain Mustafa, said to him, "Since we share the same name, from now on I shall call you Mustafa Kemal ("Mr. Perfection"), so that there shall be some distinction between us." Henceforth he was known as Mustafa Kemal.

After graduating from secondary school, Mustafa Kemal entered the Ottoman Military Academy, graduating in 1905 and commissioned as a captain. In this period of defeat after defeat for the Ottoman armies his abilities became more and more apparent. He successfully ended a rebellion in the province of Syria and restored Ottoman authority over Libya, in northern Africa. His greatest military successes were achieved during World War I. He led the successful defense of the Straits against a combined British-Anzac (Australian and New Zealand Army Corps) expeditionary force that landed at Gallipoli in 1915. It was the first Ottoman victory over European armies in more than a century.

Turkey's oldest living war veteran, aged 103, fought in the Gallipoli campaign and wears a large gold medal on the front of his jacket as proof.

A recent visitor to Edremit, a small city near the Aegean coast where he lives, reported that he sits in front of the popular Café Zeki on the city's main square every day, regaling visitors with tales of the campaign.

The Gallipoli victory, plus a number of successful fighting retreats organized by Mustafa Kemal in the face of enormous odds, made him a national hero. By the war's end he was a *paşa* (general) and had become almost the only commander in whom the Mehmets could take pride.

At this crucial stage in Turkish history destiny again reached out to touch Mustafa Kemal. His successes and his outspoken views about the need for change had made him many enemies, especially at the court of the Sultan. Certain courtiers began whispering in the Sultan's ear that "this Paşa is a dangerous man. He may be plotting to seize power." By coincidence the British commander at Constantinople had warned the Sultan that pending a peace treaty, an Ottoman officer was needed in Anatolia to restore order and keep peace between Turk and Greek. The courtiers urged the Sultan to send Mustafa Kemal on this assignment. It would get him out of the way and reassure the European powers of the Ottoman government's desire to cooperate.

The Sultan agreed, and Mustafa Kemal was ordered to Anatolia with the purposely vague title of Inspector-General. His enemies assumed that they had seen the last of him, but the new Inspector-General had other ideas. He and his friends had talked endlessly through the dark nights after the armistice, mapping Turkey's future as they drank cup after cup of Turkish coffee. They were agreed that the solution was a fresh start, a Turkey vastly different from the old one. It would be developed in Anatolia, far from Constantinople; to Kemal and his friends Constantinople was a symbol for Ottoman decadence and defeat, a city associated with European control and influence.

The War for National Liberation

The struggle to bring this new Turkey into existence took place in two stages. The first stage was the liberation of Anatolia from foreign occupation. It lasted for three years (1919–1922), ending in the recognition of Turkey as an independent nation. The second stage was longer and more difficult, since it involved the liberation of the Turkish people from ignorance, poverty, political backwardness, and reactionary conservatism. In some respects this stage is still incomplete, but the fact that modern Turkey is a republic operating under constitutional principles indicates how far the Turks have progressed in a little over sixty years.

When Mustafa Kemal arrived in Anatolia in 1919, he found a situation tailor-made for his plans. The Anatolian Turks were angry over defeat, over foreign occupation, and especially angry over the Greek invasion. He went straight to work, organizing an army and political committees to spread nationalism among city dwellers and villagers alike. Two important meetings were held in the cities of Sivas and Erzurum in eastern Anatolia to formulate the nationalist program. The result was the National Pact *(Milli-i-Misak)*.

It proclaimed in ringing terms the independence of Anatolia and eastern Thrace as an indivisible national unit, sovereign and free, ruled by a government chosen freely by the people, with equal justice under law for all persons including minorities. The provisions of the Pact were later incorporated into the Turkish constitution.

When news of the Pact reached Constantinople, Mustafa Kemal's enemies convinced the Sultan to declare him a rebel. A price was put on his head. The Grand Mufti, the chief Ottoman religious leader, issued a *fetva* saying that it was the duty of Muslims to kill the rebels. But Mustafa Kemal stayed well beyond the reach of the Sultan's forces.

The headquarters for the war of liberation was Angora (Ankara), chosen for its central location and remoteness from Constantinople. Today it is a huge modern city, but when the Paşa arrived it was a town of about 20,000 people living in mud-brick houses crammed together like a rabbit warren around a half-ruined citadel. There were no streets, only steep lanes of rough cobbles. It had been the site of a great defeat of an Ottoman Sultan by Central Asian Tatar warriors in 1402; this was its only claim to fame. It did have a railroad line built by the Germans during World War I for transportation of troops toward the Russian front. It was a frontier place with almost no hotels or other amenities.

From this unlikely headquarters Mustafa Kemal launched one of the most unusual wars of liberation in history. It was unusual in that the nationalists opposed not only foreign occupation forces but also those of their own government. As noted above, Mustafa Kemal was officially a rebel with a price on his head. In the eyes of the world, the nationalists' capture of towns and cities from their Ottoman garrisons constituted a rebellion against legal authority and therefore a violation of the armistice agreement.

Meanwhile the European powers completed the Treaty of Sèvres. Its terms were harsh. Thrace and western Anatolia would be given to Greece along with the offshore Aegean islands. Armenia and Kurdistan, in eastern Anatolia, would become independent. France and Italy were given southeastern Anatolia and the Mediterranean coast respectively as protectorates. Only Constantinople and its hinterland, plus a strip of Black Sea coast, would remain as sovereign Ottoman territory.

Although the Sultan had little choice when he signed the treaty, many people turned against him. It seemed to them that he, rather than Kemal, was the real traitor. More and more converts joined the nationalists. Particularly in Constantinople young men and women from the best families formed their own nationalist committees in secret. Their parents remained loyal to the Sultan—he was still the lord of Islam. But this attitude did not stop the young people. They organized a secret arms lift to help Mustafa Kemal.

It must have been quite an adventure. Late at night, while their families slept, the young people slipped from their homes, clad in gray wool jackets and trousers and tennis shoes, like a pack of ghostly gray wolves. They crept through silent streets to the Constantinople arsenals. The arsenal gates were opened by loyal confederates, and the pack slipped in, loading rifles, ammunition, machine guns, even dismantled cannon, into peasant carts heaped high with hay, then hauling the carts down to the harbor and aboard freighters bound for the port of Inebolu on the Black Sea. When the ships headed up the Bosporus later in the morning, the British guards never guessed that beneath the piles of hay and boxes of produce lay tons of military equipment for Mustafa Kemal's forces. Nor did the British surmise that most of the "aged" peasants aboard, wrapped in long gray cloaks, were young officers going to join the nationalists.

At the port of Inebolu another drama of the war for liberation unfolded. From there a rough cart track led up through rugged mountains and along the lonely plateau to Angora 200 miles (320 km.) away. Along this track plodded a human chain—old men, women, and children, with some Mehmets and the young officers from Constantinople interspersed among them, carrying the smuggled weapons to nationalist headquarters. This human chain saved Mustafa Kemal's ill-equipped army from almost certain defeat at the hands of the Greeks.

Meanwhile the Greek army continued its advance inland toward Angora, confident in its superiority over the Turks in numbers and equipment. But the Turks felt they were fighting for the "sacred soil" of Anatolia. They retreated slowly, battling the Greeks every step of the way and drawing them ever farther from their familiar Aegean into the waterless, sunbaked Anatolian interior.

The Turks made their final stand in August 1921 on the Sakarya River, one of the great rivers of central Anatolia. It is a natural barrier, flowing in a series of sweeping curves from its source near ancient Gordium to the Black Sea. For much of its course it flows through deep gorges, providing the Turks with a strong defensive position, while the Greeks were in unfamiliar territory, suffering from exhaustion, heat, and thirst.

The Battle of the Sakarya lasted twenty-two days, one of the longest engagements in recorded history. Halide Edib said that it was like watching two great dragons coiled around each other and around the coils of the river in a fight to the death. But in the end the Mehmets prevailed. The Greek army retreated all the way back to Smyrna, destroying everything in its path as the Turks followed in hot pursuit. At Smyrna the Greek soldiers climbed aboard ships hastily summoned

Greek refugees flee Smyrna (Izmir) in 1922 as the city burns.   AP/Wide World Photos from Greece to evacuate them. As they looked back across the dark Aegean toward their broken dream, they could see clearly the smoke and flames rising from the burning city, much of it destroyed by the Turks in revenge.

The defeat of the Greeks freed the nationalists from any further direct military danger. But foreign powers still occupied large parts of Anatolia. Mustafa Kemal now turned to diplomacy. Although the Sultan was still in theory head of the government and Constantinople remained the capital, Kemal increasingly was recognized by these foreign powers as the real leader of the Turkish state. In 1921, for example, he signed a treaty of friendship and cooperation on behalf of the nationalists with the new Soviet government of Lenin and Stalin.

After this treaty had been signed, Turkish and Soviet forces converged on the Republic of Armenia, which had been formed by Armenian leaders in their traditional homeland with promises of support from U.S. President Woodrow Wilson and British Prime Minister David Lloyd George. These promises were not kept, resulting in yet another tragedy for the Armenians. Most of the remaining Armenians in Anatolia fled across the border into the new Armenian Soviet Socialist Republic, set up by the Soviet government as one of its member republics.

Next, Kemal signed agreements with France and Italy leading to withdrawal of their occupation forces. With most of Anatolia under its control, Mustafa Kemal's army moved slowly northward toward Constantinople, still controlled by the British. British and Turkish forces faced each other once again, near the ruins of Troy. But this time there was no desire for war—British soldiers even helped a Turkish unit string barbed wire before its trenches because a Turkish general was coming to inspect its defenses.

There was now no reason for further delay in settling Turkey's affairs. The Treaty of Sèvres was annulled, and the European powers met with Mustafa Kemal's representative, Ismet Inönü, in Lausanne,

The signing of the Lausanne Treaty as seen in a contemporary cartoon. Leaders of France, England, and Italy oversee Ismet Inönü holding the pen. Reprinted by permission of Westview Press from *Turkey: Coping with Crisis*, by George Harris, © Westview Press, Boulder, Colorado, 1985.

Switzerland, in 1922–1923, to hammer out the details of a peace treaty. The Treaty of Lausanne (1923) recognized Turkey as a sovereign nation within the borders specified in the National Pact. A later treaty, signed in Montreux, Switzerland, in 1936, confirmed Turkish sovereignty over the Bosporus and the Dardanelles (Straits).

Father of the Turks

At the age of forty-two, Mustafa Kemal seemed to be at the peak of his career as the leader of a newly independent Turkish state. But inwardly he knew that the real struggle lay ahead, the struggle to lift the Turkish people out of centuries of lethargy, poverty, and ignorance. Although most Turks agreed with Kemal that the country should be independent, they agreed on little else. Some of those who had fought with him in the war of liberation feared he might have ideas about becoming a dictator—or worse yet, founding a new dynasty. For this reason Mustafa

Kemal moved slowly and carefully, step by step with his plans.

After independence a new Grand National Assembly had been elected as the responsible legislative body for the republic. Kemal served both as its president and what we would call its floor leader in carrying out his program for change into legislative form. The first step was to eliminate the office of Sultan. This was not difficult, since the Sultan was discredited for his surrender to European powers and because of his inability to rule effectively. On October 29, 1923, the Assembly formally abolished the sultanate and declared Turkey a republic.

Next, Mustafa Kemal set out to establish a republican form of government. Although the country was officially a republic, the idea of republicanism was not easy for the Turks to comprehend. They were used to an autocratic government that did their thinking for them and made all decisions except a few personal ones. Kemal proposed to change that. New laws were passed providing for an elected president, with a prime minister and cabinet responsible to the president. As expected, Mustafa Kemal was unanimously elected as Turkey's first president.

Mustafa Kemal did not believe that the Turks were ready for a multiparty democratic political system or even a two-party system such as exists in the United States. The first step in his view was to develop a sense of political responsibility and participation. He set up the country's first European-style political party, the Republican People's Party (RPP). Although during his lifetime it was little more than a vehicle for his programs and ideas, the RPP was a sound starting place toward political participation.

Although Mustafa Kemal ruled more as a dictator than as an elected president, he believed that his role was to guide and teach rather than simply to tell the people what they must do. He took literally the Turkish proverb "The world is a pot, and man is its ladle." He was constantly stirring new ideas into the pot, reshaping society in a modern image, encouraging people to slough off old ways that seemed to interfere with progress. He did not tolerate criticism, and when he was convinced that a reform needed to be made, he would brook no opposition. A number of his old comrades turned against him when they felt he was moving too fast or undermining the Islamic traditions and values that held Turkish society together.

Some of these ideas may seem strange to us now, but they were important at the time. One was the matter of place names. Turkish cities were renamed to purge them of foreign elements—Angora became Ankara and Smyrna Izmir, while Constantinople lost not only its status as Turkey's capital but reappeared on maps as Istanbul.

Mustafa Kemal also decided that it was time for all Turks to have last names. In Ottoman days they had only one name, whispered in a baby's ear by its father at birth. But in the modern world they would need last names to distinguish the various Ahmets, Mehmets, Mustafas, and Hasans from each other. The Assembly started things off by giving Mustafa Kemal the surname Atatürk ("father of the Turks," in a tutorial rather than a parental sense). Ismet, his right-hand man and successor as president took the surname Inönü from the place of the first Turkish victory over the Greeks. There were some amusing results as people hunted through dictionaries and other reference works to find interesting and colorful surnames.

One of the most significant long-term changes in Turkish life initiated by Atatürk was in the area of language. Ottoman Turkish was a hodgepodge of Arabic, Persian, Turkish, and European words, written in several different scripts and incomprehensible to all but a few educated people. It was totally unsuited to the development of the new Turkish nation in its relations with other nations. Atatürk called a meeting of linguistic scholars and asked them how long it would take people to

Atatürk teaching the new form of the Turkish language.   Barbara K. Walker

learn to read and write modern Turkish purged of most foreign words and written in an alphabet of Latin characters. The scholars said fifteen years. "Very well," replied Atatürk, "you have three months." At the end of that period all newspapers, street signs, public notices, books, and magazines appeared written in the new Turkish, from left to right and in Latin characters. The new Turkish was phonetic; each letter had a single pronunciation, and as soon as people learned the sounds they could put words together. For a while many persons could not read the printed word. Some religious leaders accused Atatürk of heresy; they said God's word in the Koran had to be in Arabic. So Atatürk took blackboard and chalk, and traveled throughout the country to give classes in the new script. "The best proof that we are Turks," he said, "is that we have our own national language."

There were other changes. Turkey joined the western world in 1926 by adopting the Gregorian calendar. The fez, the traditional tall, brimless, red conical cap with a tassel worn by male Turks, was prohibited by law. Atatürk had once been laughed at on a visit to Europe for wearing one, and to him it was a symbol of Turkish backwardness. Men began wearing panama hats, visored felt caps, skullcaps, or even beanies to satisfy the desire for some sort of head covering.

Another new law outlawed polygamy—no more harems—and established procedures for civil divorce. Although the veil was not officially outlawed, it was discouraged; led by bold spirits such as Halide Edib, Turkish women began to turn away from the veil. They began to work in offices, and not only wear European clothes, but also create new fashion designs. As a result Turkey is emerging as a worldwide center for fashion today.

The Death of Atatürk

By the fall of 1938 Mustafa Kemal Atatürk had been President of the republic for fifteen years. He was fifty-seven and suffering from cirrhosis of the liver. On October 29 he was scheduled to go to Ankara from

---

Hats

Atatürk once visited Kastamonu, a city whose population was known to be very conservative, and told a crowd, "I've brought you some nice presents. They are called hats. They are much more suitable for protection against the sun and rain than the fez."

Atatürk (holding his hat, center), Celal Bayar (fourth from the left), and other leaders of the republic at a public function. Atatürk liked to mingle with his people and be readily accessible to all. Turkish Tourism Office

Istanbul to address the Grand National Assembly on the anniversary of independence. But he was too ill; one of his chief lieutenants, Celal Bayar (Turkey's third president), read his speech for him.

Atatürk spent his last days aboard a yacht anchored in the Bosporus, where he could be cooler than in the city. Here he continued to direct the affairs of the republic from his sickbed. The most important decision to be made was the choice of a successor. It had to be someone who shared his vision of a free, proud, progressive Turkey, preferably someone who had been at his side from the beginning of the struggle for liberation.

His choice was Ismet Inönü, the old campaigner and chief of staff in the battle with the Greeks. It was to be Atatürk's last official act, made just hours before his death. Mustafa Kemal Atatürk died on November 10, 1938, at 9:05 A.M. The time of his death is still observed with a minute of silence throughout Turkey. When the news of his death was announced, an entire nation broke down. Hundreds of thousands of stolid, disciplined, unemotional people broke down and wept as they followed his coffin through the streets of Istanbul. It was put aboard a cruiser for the journey up the coast to the railhead at Izmit, then taken by train to Ankara for his final resting place. No Sultan ever had such a hold on the hearts and minds of his people as did Atatürk. He never sought the absolute power of a Sultan, and his goals were simple and straightforward—a sovereign Turkish nation united within internationally recognized borders, a nation capable of ruling itself democratically. His achievement laid the foundation so solidly that others could build upon it.

One Government, Three Republics

We have accomplished many and great tasks in a
short time. The greatest of these is the
Turkish Republic, the basis of which is Turkish
heroism and courage.

Atatürk, Speech on the tenth anniversary

of the Republic, 1933

Atatürk's great strength was in his concern for his country's future. Although he was not always right in his decisions, he was unusual among leaders of newly independent nations in concentrating not so much on enhancing his own position as in preparing the way for others to follow and carry on his work. He was particularly supportive of Turkey's youth. In his most famous speech, known as the Great Speech (1927), he spoke to them with pride of his hopes for them, and of entrusting to them the future of the republic:

O Turkish youth!
Your first duty is to defend forever the independence of the Republic!
The strength you may need is there,
In the noble blood that flows through your veins!

In the years since Atatürk's death Turks have often disagreed, sometimes violently, over the means of developing an effective system of
democratic government, but they are generally in agreement about the
long-term goals that Atatürk sought. Turkey today continues to work
toward democracy, although it has not yet achieved a true representative
system of government. Atatürk was undoubtedly correct in his insistence on moving slowly away from the autocratic system under which
Turks had lived for six hundred years. In this sense he was an astute
judge of Turkish character. However, a serious weakness in his leadership during his fifteen years in office was his failure to move the people
away from their traditional dependence on a dictatorial father figure.
It is fair to say that he became so enamored of the father-figure image
of himself that he did not allow the people to make mistakes or to
question his decisions once they had been made. What he sought was
good for the country in general, but there were no checks and balances
built into the relationship between leader and people, legislature and
president. The legacy of Atatürk with its strengths and weaknesses can
be seen in the progression of government through three distinct periods
of republicanism and the transitions between them, marked by military
intervention.

Atatürk's Legacy

There have been three republics in modern Turkish history, roughly
identical in form. The first republic continued after Atatürk's death
under the single-party system until 1950, when it was replaced by a
two-party system. The second and third republics were separated by
periods of military rule. However, each intervention by the military
ended with the restoration of civilian government, due to the military's
commitment to Atatürk's goal of civil democracy.

Atatürk defined his political program in the form of six principles, the "Six Arrows" of the Republican People's Party (RPP). They are: Republicanism, Nationalism, Populism, Etatism, Secularism, and Revolutionism. The struggle to remain true to these principles has preoccupied Turkish leaders for the last fifty years. The first three arrows have presented fewer problems, although populism (the establishment of a system of many parties representing the people's interests) has yet to be achieved. Etatism (state control of the economy) has become an obstacle to national economic development. Secularism has come under attack by Islamic fundamentalists concerned with restoring Islam to what they believe is its proper place in Turkish social and political life.

Inönü Takes Over

Ismet Inönü, the republic's second president, was almost the antithesis of Atatürk—patient, plodding, often accused of having no imagination, painstaking in detail and prudent to a fault. Yet Inönü not only held the nation together in the difficult days of World War II, he also presided over the establishment of a two-party system.

The Republic under Inönü

The first republic spanned the Atatürk and Inönü presidencies, with little change in the political system. However, World War II brought many problems. Although Turkey stayed neutral until near the end of the war, the cost of keeping a million men under arms to defend the nation strained its resources to the limit. Inflation soared, and shortages of such basic necessities as flour, sugar, salt, and cooking oil created a large black market. A special wartime tax to raise funds for military equipment angered many people. It fell heaviest on non-Muslim businesspeople, but because of its arbitrary nature it seemed to symbolize for all that the one-party system was no longer good for Turkey.

The first opposition political party was formed in 1924 by some of Atatürk's associates who disagreed with him on policy, and a second was formally established with his support in 1930. However, neither party lasted long. Associates who had been involved in the opposition movement were sometimes arrested and jailed or purged from the government.

By the end of World War II it had become apparent to Inönü that change was needed in the political system. Taking to heart the Turkish proverb "If the times don't suit you, make sure you suit the times," Inönü declared in 1946 that a two-party system was needed and would help Turkey gain the support of the Western democracies against the new threat from the Soviet Union. Several members of the RPP took him at his word. In 1946 they formed the Democratic Party (DP). Two of its leaders were Celal Bayar, a banker, and Adnan Menderes, a wealthy landowner.

Inönü expected that the new party would serve at most as a sort of "loyal opposition," but the party grew more rapidly than he or anyone else had expected. The Democrats made a strong showing in the 1946 elections, and in 1950 the party won a large majority of seats in the Assembly. It was Turkey's first free, secret election. Celal Bayar became president and Adnan Menderes Prime Minister, while Inönü gracefully shifted to a new role as leader of the opposition.

The Menderes Era, 1950–1960

The Democratic Party was Turkey's first mass popular party, representing a cross-section of Turkish society. Not only did it hold a majority in the National Assembly, but also Menderes became popular by estab-

A pottery caravan in Anatolia, near Konya.   Doranne Jacobson

lishing a close alliance with the United States. The alliance brought American aid in large amounts, equipment to modernize the army, new factories and roads and agricultural projects. Many isolated villages were linked to the outside world by road for the first time in their history. The old images of rural Turkey—the schoolmaster on his donkey, the peasant in his cart riding like Gordius to market—began to disappear, replaced by the Ford truck, the John Deere tractor, and the battered passenger car crammed with excited waving Turks on their way to town.

Unfortunately, the Democrats were no more willing to share power than their predecessors had been. The Turks had yet to develop the tradition of open debate and compromise that is rooted in democratic systems such as those of the United States and Great Britain. Instead, the Menderes regime worked to undermine its opposition through repressive laws.

In 1960, an election year, the Menderes government decided it had enough popular support to eliminate the RPP and return Turkey to the single-party system. A law was passed setting up a special Democratic Party investigating committee to examine "political activity." Its definition of political activity was broad. For example, two men who stopped to shake hands on the street could have been arrested for an "unauthorized political meeting," and probably would have been had they been RPP members.

Immediately before the election the regime tightened the screws. A ban was imposed on political meetings, the press was censored, and opposition candidates were detained, often on flimsy grounds, to keep them from campaigning. Newspapers and magazines that published articles about the opposition were confiscated. Menderes talked openly of an end to democracy.

Menderes's statements were perhaps not intended to be taken seriously, but unfortunately for him they aroused great concern on the part of the army. Although Atatürk had spent much of his professional life in the military and ruled the republic as an authoritarian leader, he was

Censorship

One such law made it a crime to publish articles critical of the government in newspapers and magazines. Editors and reporters were arrested so often that a popular cartoon of the time featured a reporter leaving his home for a party dressed in a tuxedo with a convict's uniform over his arm.

determined that the army should not involve itself in politics or interfere with the legitimate actions of civilian governments. The only exception would be in a case where the republic itself seemed to be in danger, either from foreign invasion or internal subversion. If either of these situations seemed about to occur, the army was obligated to intervene to preserve Turkish democracy. Atatürk envisaged the role of the army as that of defender of the state but not its overlord. When the danger had passed, army leaders were equally obligated to restore civilian government.

In May 1960 it seemed to army leaders that Menderes had become a threat to Turkey's democracy. True to their mission and their belief in the ideals of Atatürk, they acted to preserve the state. On May 27 they carried out a bloodless coup. Menderes, Bayar, and hundreds of DP members were arrested on charges of treason, and the party was dissolved.

May 27 is now a Turkish national holiday, known as Revolutionary Day because it ushered in the Second Republic.

The Second Republic

The May 1961 revolution represented a new start for Turkey. Menderes and several close associates were hanged, recalling the grim Turkish proverb "Even the tallest tree has an axe waiting at its foot." The army leaders were determined that the abuses of power of his regime would not be repeated. A new constitution was approved in 1961. It included a Bill of Rights similar to the one in the U.S. Constitution. A special court, somewhat similar to the U.S. Supreme Court, was set up to judge the legality of laws and try cases involving government officials.

Although the DP was outlawed, army leaders allowed other parties

Süleyman Demirel making a campaign speech in the 1970's.   Richard Kalvar/Magnum

to form in preparation for an early restoration of civilian government. The new Justice Party, formed by former DP members, quickly emerged as the leading opposition party, while the RPP continued to lose ground despite the personal popularity of Inönü. However, neither of the two major parties was able to win a clear majority in the parliamentary elections of the 1960's and 1970's. A number of smaller parties were formed; they held the balance of power because the major parties had to have their support in order to carry out legislation.

Atatürk and his two immediate successors had been strong presidents, taking an active part in government. But under the 1961 constitution the job became largely a ceremonial one.

In the late 1960's Turkey experienced a brief period of political stability, brought about largely by economic prosperity. Süleyman Demirel, head of the Justice Party, became Prime Minister, and Ismet Inönü once again retired to the opposition benches in the National Assembly at the age of eighty-eight. Inönü died in 1973 at the age of ninety-six; his old opponent Celal Bayar, who was pardoned in 1965, managed to outlive him, dying in 1986 at the age of one hundred and four!

Civil Violence in the 1970's

The period from about 1968 to 1980 is another that the Turks would like to forget. Many a black page was turned as Turk fought Turk, class was pitted against class, party against party, family member against family member. The violence stemmed from a number of causes. One was the coming of age of a new generation that challenged its elders and questioned government policies, much as many young Americans did during the Vietnam War. Turkish university students were in the forefront of the violence. They had learned about Marxism-Leninism and other radical philosophies in their course work. Fired up by their radical professors, they became convinced that social injustice in all its forms—unemployment, repression, poverty, hunger, and other social ills—were the results of government policies that were backed by most adults, who cared only for material success. As the economy floundered, unions were suppressed, and Turkey fell on hard times in the 1970's, more and more Turkish young people formed militant antigovernment organizations.

Another factor that fostered the growth of civil violence arose from the inability of the major political parties to cooperate. Increasingly, groups within the parties broke away to form separate splinter parties. As a result, government was often paralyzed as fistfights between deputies and shouting matches in the National Assembly replaced responsi-

Workers climb over an army tank in one of Turkey's many protests during the 1970's.
AP/Wide World Photo

ble lawmaking. A Turkish journalist wrote at the time: "It was as if some force had tampered with the gears and brakes of the Turkish merry-go-round and the whole contraption began visibly to spin out of control."

In this crisis the nation looked for a new Atatürk, but the grim face of the founder of the republic that stared down at them from portraits on the walls of banks, cafés, and public buildings was of little help. Not only were the major parties bitterly divided, but also their leaders seemed to be engaged in a kind of personal gladiatorial combat.

The lack of leadership prompted revolutionary groups to turn to violence to achieve their goal of changing the political system. A leftist

An old rural couple still has the head of a Gray Wolf attached to their house for good luck.   Maury Englander

terrorist group, the Turkish Peoples' Liberation Army, pulled off a series of spectacular bank robberies, kidnapings and assassinations of public figures, and sabotage, in support of their objective of armed revolution and the establishment of a Socialist government. The far right formed a political party, the NSP (National Salvation Party), modeled on the Fascists in Italy. The NSP had its underground terrorist organization, the Gray Wolves.

The gray wolf is associated with ancient legends of the Turkish people. According to legend the Turks first appeared in history as a troop of horsemen, riding westward across the Asian steppes, led by a gray wolf. Atatürk used the symbol to rally the Turks after World War I.

This terrorist group countered what they perceived as a threat to the nation with random murders of prominent leftists and bombings of theaters and cafés. Their leader, Colonel Alpaslan Turkeş, told a new group of recruits: "I have embraced this cause; I am going ahead and heeding nothing. Follow me. If I should turn back, shoot me. Shoot anyone who joins the cause and then turns back."

Unfortunately the struggle between left and right, liberation fighters and Gray Wolves, began to affect more and more innocent people. By mid-1979 the death toll was averaging twenty persons a day. No one was safe; whatever their walk of life, people were gunned down in restaurants, businesses, bus lines, or wherever they happened to be. Often, however, the terrorists chose particular victims, such as newspaper editors who had challenged their ideas in print or exposed their deadly ideology.

The Third Republic

By 1980 Turkish society seemed paralyzed by violence and disorder; the political system had almost ceased to function. Until then military

---

Mehmet Ali Ağça

Abdi Ipekçi, editor of the influential daily newspaper *Milliyet*, was assassinated in February 1979. The assassin, Mehmet Ali Ağça, a member of the Gray Wolves, was later caught and sentenced to death for the crime. He escaped from prison under unclear circumstances and made his way to Rome, where he tried unsuccessfully to assassinate Pope John Paul II. At this writing he is in prison in Italy.

leaders had stayed out of the civil conflict, although they issued stern warnings to political leaders from time to time to halt the violence. In September 1980 they intervened for the third time in the republic's history. Army leaders concluded that the civil violence was tearing the country apart.

This time the army leaders were determined to make no mistakes, and they were in no hurry to restore civilian government. The National Assembly was suspended and martial law imposed throughout the country. Leaders of the major political parties were jailed while army and police units rounded up hundreds of both left- and right-wing terrorists. Labor unions were ordered disbanded, and early in 1981 all existing political parties were abolished. Justice Party and RPP leaders were also banned from politics for ten years. (The ban was lifted in 1987 following a national referendum that confirmed an earlier decision by the National Assembly.)

The coup was immensely popular with the majority of the population, and also with Turkey's North Atlantic Treaty Organization allies, who had watched the chaos of the 1970's with growing concern. Within the country people greeted each other on the streets for the first time in years, mixed in restaurants, and went to the movies without fear. The army Chief of Staff, General Kenan Evren, was even compared with Atatürk, although the General disclaimed any such role and repeatedly stressed earlier pledges that civilian government would be restored "at the appropriate time."

Thus far Evren and his associates have kept their word. A new constitution, Turkey's third, was approved in 1982. It extends the President's term of office to seven years and gives him much greater powers than in the recent past, comparable to those of Atatürk and Inönü. A national referendum elected Evren President in the same year, assuring continuity for the regime.

Turgut Özal

Although previously known for his work on the economic
stabilization program that the military leaders initiated in 1980 to
shore up the Turkish economy, Özal seems to have taken to politics
like a duck to water. His round face, schoolmaster's glasses, and
thick black mustache have become as familiar to Turkish TV
viewers as the fatherly President Evren, who criticized the
Motherland leader during the campaign for his "unseemly" political
tactics.

However, the Evren government's record in human rights has been
less commendable. As recently as 1985 Amnesty International estimated that 180,000 political prisoners were still held in jail from the
1980 coup, many of them under harsh conditions, with torture of
prisoners being systematic and widespread. The harshest treatment is
reportedly reserved for Kurdish prisoners, many of whom are held in
the maximum-security prison at Diyarbakir (a forbidding city in any
case, isolated behind its grim black basalt walls along the Tigris).

Political life has slowly returned to a more normal status. The generals said they would allow new political parties to form, and set a
November 1983 date for elections to a 400-member National Assembly,
enlarged from the previous one. Three parties entered candidates for the
new Assembly. The odds-on favorite and preference of army leaders was
the National Democracy Party, headed by a retired general. But the
Motherland Party, led by Turgut Özal, an economist, surprised every-
one with a stunning victory at the polls. (Özal and his associates ran an
American-style campaign with a media blitz, whistle stops, and personal

appearances by the candidate in remote villages as well as cities.)

Özal was reelected Prime Minister by another large majority in November 1987, giving him another four years in office. Three new parties that were allowed to participate in the election were the True Path, successor to the Justice Party and headed by Süleyman Demirel; the Social Democratic Party, led by Ismet Inönü's son Erdal, a physicist and university rector; and the Free Democrats formed out of the RPP and headed by Bülent Ecevit, ex-RPP chief.

The 1987 elections outlined the probable course of national politics for the foreseeable future—although nothing is certain given the volatile nature of Turkish society. The Motherland Party's share of the popular vote dropped, but it retained its 2-to-1 majority in the National Assembly, which was expanded to 450 members. The party won 292 seats. The Social Democrats finished a distant second with ninety-nine, and True Path farther behind with fifty-nine. Ecevit's party finished last and promptly broke up as its leader retired from public life. With small ideologically motivated parties and violence-advocating splinter groups excluded from politics, and reasonably clear distinctions between the Motherland Party and its rivals, the Third Republic should show more orderly progress than the first two—especially with five generals looking over Mr. Özal's shoulder.

Turkey and the World

We come from the East, we go to the West.
Turkish proverb

Turkey's relations with other countries since the founding of the republic have been determined mainly by geography. The country has had to fend off powerful neighbors; it is determined to remain independent of foreign control; and it wants to become more closely aligned with Western Europe. Most Turks have generally supported government foreign policy regardless of which party was in power at the time. As a result the nation's external policies have been less controversial and more consistent than its internal politics. It has been much easier to develop a consensus on foreign policy moves, including such actions as the 1974 Turkish troop landings at Cyprus, which was criticized even by Turkey's allies, than it has been to establish a workable political system.

Atatürk's Foreign Policy

With the establishment of the republic Atatürk set out to break away from the Ottoman past. His goal was to base the new Turkey's relations

Hatay and Syria

The one exception to Atatürk's peaceful foreign policy was annexation of the Hatay region, located just outside Anatolia at the northeast end of the Mediterranean. This region had been included in French-controlled Syria in the division of Ottoman territories after World War I. However, it had a large Turkish population that agitated for inclusion in the republic from 1923 on. The League of Nations sponsored a plebiscite in 1938 to determine the wishes of the inhabitants. The results showed a majority in favor of annexation by Turkey. However, Syria has never accepted the loss of what it considers legitimate Syrian territory. This is one reason for the generally bad relations between Turkey and Syria that exist to this day.

The view from Mardin extends into Syria. In climate and architecture this part of Turkey is reminiscent of the Middle East. Joseph Lawton

with its neighbors and all countries on mutual respect and staying out of each other's internal affairs. Atatürk renounced aggression and territorial expansion beyond the nation's borders as defined in the Treaty of Lausanne.

Atatürk set the tone for foreign policy in his famous phrase "Peace at home, peace in the world." The phrase appears in the preamble to the 1982 constitution and has guided Turkey's relations with other nations up to the present time. But peace in the world was not simply an idealistic policy developed in the hope that nations would automatically work together for the betterment of human society. Atatürk was

a realist; he and his successors sometimes took initiatives that appeared warlike rather than peaceful in working to achieve peace, just as all nations have done from time to time. Thus, the Inönü government declared war on Nazi Germany, and the Menderes government joined forces with other countries in sending troops to Korea in the 1950's to help that country resist a Communist invasion.

Atatürk sought to avoid the entangling alliances that had trapped the Ottomans into involvement in World War I and eventually cost them their empire. In the 1930's he sought to cultivate good relations with both the European democracies and the Fascist regimes of Germany and

Italy. Turkey had close economic relations with Nazi Germany and was dependent on the Germans for military equipment and spare parts for the armed forces. Thus, when World War II broke out it might have been expected that Turkey would side with Germany. But President Inönü resisted German pressures and instead chose a policy of strict neutrality, although perhaps favoring the Western allies—thus German requests for transit rights to ship arms to pro-German troops operating in the Middle East were consistently refused. In February 1945 Turkey declared war on Germany, although it did not engage in actual hostilities. It could be said that the declaration at such a late date was an enlightened form of self-interest, but it nonetheless put Turkey in a position to become one of the the founding members of the United Nations.

The Long Relationship with Russia

The country's relations with its northern neighbor go back many centuries. At one time the Ottomans ruled much of southern Russia. As the empire began to weaken, Russia regained parts of its territory so that by the time of World War I Turks and Russians had fought thirteen separate wars, nearly all of them ending in defeat for the Sultan's forces.

Russia's primary goal was control of Constantinople and the Straits to ensure access to the Mediterranean for its fleet. But each time the Russians seemed about to the reach their goal, European powers, mainly England and France, intervened on behalf of the Sultan to keep the empire from falling under Russian control.

World War I brought about a change in the relationship. The Russian government was overthrown by a revolution in 1917, and when the Communists gained power after a bloody civil war, they were isolated from the rest of Europe. England and France, their wartime allies, turned on them and supported various groups that were trying to over-throw the new Communist regime. The Turkish nationalists, led by Mustafa Kemal, found themselves also isolated and under attack, giving the two regimes something in common for the first time in the long history of Turkish-Russian relations. Soviet aid was instrumental in building up the army of liberation, and as noted earlier, the 1921 treaty of friendship led to joint Turkish-Soviet action to destroy the independent republic of Armenia.

The treaty also defined the Turkish-Soviet border along lines that have not changed. The far-eastern Anatolian districts of Kars and Arda-han, taken from Turkey in 1878, were returned to Turkish control, while Batumi, an oil port and refinery site on the Black Sea, and thus important to the Soviet oil industry, remained in Soviet territory.

Although Atatürk had been grateful for Soviet help in the War of Liberation, he viewed the treaty as a protective measure. He had no use for Communism, which he considered to be Russian expansionism in another form. He saw the Soviet experiments in agricultural collectives and forced industrialization as doomed to failure because they were against the welfare of the people. Other than some economic aid there was little contact between the two countries during his lifetime.

By the end of World War II the situation was different. The Soviet Union had become a major power, with a strong army and an aggressive foreign policy aimed at achieving historic Russian goals. Joseph Stalin, the Soviet dictator, demanded the return of Kars and Ardahan, and joint Turkish-Soviet control of the Straits, as the price for renewal of the 1921 treaty.

The reaction to these demands was a wave of nationalist feeling. President Inönü told the Grand National Assembly, "We shall live with honor and die with honor," and the Speaker of the Assembly declared, "If the Russians insist on their demand, we shall fight to the last Turk."

These were bold words, but they might have been of little avail against Soviet tanks. Fortunately for Turkey, the spread of Soviet aggression had alarmed the U.S. and its allies. Soviet-backed Communist regimes had seized power in the central European countries, and in addition to Turkey, Greece was threatened by Communist subversion. In 1947 President Harry Truman announced the Truman Doctrine in a message to Congress. The Doctrine authorized large-scale military and economic aid to Greece and Turkey as a means of countering the Communist threat. American military equipment poured into Turkey. Stalin declared that the country was becoming a base for American operations against the Soviet Union and threatened to invade.

However, the Soviet leader was not ready to risk a new war, this time with the powerful United States, over the Straits. The Soviet threat receded further in 1952 when Turkey became a member of the North Atlantic Treaty Organization (NATO), ensuring military support from Western Europe.

After Stalin's death in 1953, Soviet leaders publicly admitted that Stalin's approach to Turkey had been a mistake. The Turks were too proud and too nationalistic, they said, to submit to such bullying tactics. Since then the Soviet Union has sought to cultivate better relations through large-scale economic aid and formal renunciation of all claims to Turkish territory. Soviet aid projects have included a steel mill at Iskenderun, a dam on the Arpaçay River along the border, and an oil refinery.

However, centuries of distrust between nations do not vanish. The Turks continue to maintain cool but distant relations with the Soviet Union, although in recent years they have allowed not only Soviet merchant vessels, but also warships, to transit the Bosporus regularly without interference. This policy has caused concern among American policymakers and created problems in the all-important relationship between the two countries.

Turks and Americans— an Uneasy Marriage

Turkish-American contacts date back to the early nineteenth century. In those days the contacts between the Ottoman Empire and the U.S. were mainly through missionaries. Church groups such as the American Mission Board, concerned about the lack of education for Christian subjects of the Sultan, established such schools as Robert College and the Syrian Protestant College, now the American University of Beirut, in Ottoman cities. Although these colleges were originally intended for Christians, in time they began to teach Muslims as well. Robert College in particular has made a significant contribution to the Turkish Republic over the years in educating many future leaders.

Turkish-American friendship was enhanced after World War I, when Admiral Mark Bristol, commander of the small American contingent sent to Constantinople with Allied occupation forces, strongly supported

The Transition

An American diplomat who served as Consul-General in Istanbul in the 1970's recalled that upon arrival at his post, "I found three employees dating back to Ottoman days. They had a combined total of about 150 years' service to the U.S. government. . . . They helped carry Turkey through the transition from empire to republic and the United States from distant friend to close ally."

(James W. Spain, *American Diplomacy in Turkey.* New York: Praeger, 1984, pp. 167–68.)

· 141 ·

Mustafa Kemal and advised the U.S. government to recognize the nationalists as the legitimate Turkish government. Admiral Bristol later founded the American hospital in Istanbul, which bears his name, and established there the first school of nursing in the country.

Turkish and American national interests converged after World War II. The U.S. effort to contain the Soviet Union through a belt of allied non-Communist nations along the Soviet border coincided with Turkey's determination to resist Stalin's demands for territory and control of the Straits.

The new close alignment seemed to indicate in the 1950's and 1960's that Turkey was well on its way to full partnership with the Western democracies, turning its back on the East. The country also broke with its Islamic Arab neighbors by recognizing the new State of Israel in 1949, signing military agreements with Greece and Yugoslavia in 1954, and in addition to NATO joining the Baghdad Pact, an alliance of non-Communist states (Turkey, Iran, Iraq, plus Britain) along the long and vulnerable southern Soviet border. American military personnel in ever-increasing numbers were assigned to airbases, missile sites, radar installations, and other American facilities leased from the Turkish government. But in time the American presence began to create problems. These foreigners were exempt from Turkish law under the Status of Forces agreement. It seemed to many Turks that the exploitive Capitulations of Ottoman times were being repeated.

American personnel were able to live much better, because of their hardship and overseas allowances, than their hosts. Thus, not only did an American sergeant earn more money than a Turkish university professor, but he also had access to the military PX with prices well below those of the Turkish market, as well as duty-free privileges for cars and household goods. The disparity in living conditions caused considerable resentment among the Turks as time went on and the standard of living gap widened.

Despite these irritants the Turkish-American friendship seemed solid, so much so that each country increasingly took the other for granted in pursuing its foreign policies. The Turks came to expect that they would be consulted in the event of a Soviet challenge to American interests that might involve them, while the United States expected that Turkey would automatically support American global strategy. But in 1962 when President John F. Kennedy ordered the removal of Jupiter intermediate ballistic missiles, which were deployed on Turkish territory, in return for removal of Soviet missiles from Cuba, he did so without first consulting Turkish leaders. Understandably, the move was a blow to national pride, especially since Turkey had supported Kennedy's willingness to stand up to the Russians.

The Cyprus Issue

The foreign policy issue that has divided Turkey and the United States and undermined the alliance more than any other is Cyprus. Cyprus, an island republic forty miles from the Turkish coast, was part of the Ottoman Empire for many centuries. During that time a sizable Turkish population settled on the island, but the majority remained Greek.

Cyprus was ceded to England in 1878 in a treaty that guaranteed British support for the Ottomans against Russia. It was governed as a British Crown Colony until 1959, when it became independent. The United States was not a party to the negotiations for independence for Cyprus. But, because both Greece and Turkey were its allies, and they were sharply divided on the issue, America had to make some hard choices. In 1964 concern over the repression of Turkish Cypriots by the Greek Cypriot majority led the Inönü government to warn Washington that it intended to intervene. President Johnson warned Inönü bluntly that if Turkey did so, the United States might reconsider its obligation to protect the Turks in the event of a Soviet invasion, which still seemed possible at that time. He added that in no case could American-made equipment be used in Cyprus.

The warning had its effect, and the Turks desisted. But when the contents of the Johnson letter were leaked to the Turkish press, there was an outcry of public resentment. Turks felt betrayed by their most trusted ally. Demonstrations in cities brought shouts of "Yankee, go home!" where only a decade earlier they had welcomed American military personnel. Many scholars believe that this was the start of anti-Americanism in Turkey.

In 1974 the Turks carried out their threat against Cyprus. A mutiny of Greek Cypriot national-guard units had overthrown the Cypriot government. The island's new leaders talked openly of *enosis* (union) with mainland Greece. Fearing that such a move would endanger the lives and civil rights of Turkish Cypriots, an expeditionary force landed on Cyprus, eventually occupying the northern third of the island.

By this time it had become apparent that in both Turkey and the United States, domestic politics affected the alliance more than traditional friendship or common interests. As the Soviet Union came to be seen as less and less of a major threat, the Turks became preoccupied with growing civil violence and political deadlock among their major parties. In the United States, Congress was pressing to regain legislative control over foreign policy in the aftermath of Watergate. Not only were members of Congress angry about the invasion, but also they objected to the use of U.S. weapons by Turkish forces in the invasion. All military aid and arms sales to Turkey were suspended. The Turkish response was tit for tat as U.S. bases were shut down and American military personnel ordered home. The deadlock lasted until 1978, when President Carter personally intervened with Congress to restore the

Turkish aid program. The American bases were reopened and arms shipments resumed in 1979.

But the close ties of earlier years clearly no longer exist. U.S. aid to Turkey has been reduced steadily in the 1980's despite Turkish pleas that more is needed to upgrade the army to meet modern standards. On its side Turkey has initiated actions designed to lessen its dependence upon the United States and to diversify its support base by such moves as aligning itself with Arab and other Islamic countries and improving relations with the Soviet Union.

Again the Armenians

In addition to the Cyprus problem, a second issue that emerged in the 1970's to affect Turkey's relations with the United States and its European allies was that of the Armenians. The spread of international terrorism and the use of violence to dramatize minority causes (such as those of the Palestinians in Israel and the Catholics in Northern Ireland) led to the development of secret Armenian terrorist organizations seeking revenge against the Turks for the Armenian massacres of 1895–1896 and 1915–1916. The best-known of these organizations is the Armenian Secret Army for the Liberation of Armenia (ASALA). ASALA goes beyond simple revenge to advocate the establishment by violent means of an independent Armenian state in eastern Anatolia. In the 1970's and early 1980's ASALA gunmen wounded or murdered a number of Turkish diplomats stationed in various countries, including the United States. ASALA agents penetrated Turkish territory on two occasions, killing or injuring scores of people in attacks at Ankara airport and the Grand Bazaar in Istanbul.

The worldwide Armenian community disavows terrorism and dissociates itself from sponsorship of ASALA. But the larger issue of Turkish

"Armenian Day"?

A proposed resolution in the House of Representatives to establish April 24 as an annual "Armenian Day" commemorating the 1915–1916 massacre of Armenians was narrowly defeated in 1987, the Reagan administration having warned Congress that approval would be a needless slap at a trusted ally. The Turks, not fully understanding the relationship between American interest groups and Congress in its foreign policy role, angrily denounced the proposal as an *official* U.S. government action, which it was not, merely reflecting the sentiments of Congressional leaders.

responsibility for the 1915–1916 deportation of Armenians from eastern Anatolia and the subsequent deaths of hundreds of thousands of them continues to haunt the republic in its relations abroad. The issue has affected Turkish-American relations, particularly due to domestic political pressure from the large Armenian community in the United States, in much the same way as American Jewish organizations use their political and financial clout to influence American policy toward Israel.

Until very recently the Turks have stubbornly maintained that the deportation and subsequent deaths of somewhere between 300,000 (their figure) and 2 million Armenians did not result from a deliberate policy of genocide, as the Armenians claim. The Turks point to the appalling wartime conditions in eastern Anatolia, where epidemic dis-

Shahnour Ushulian, an Armenian bride from Afyonkarahisar, taken about 1910. Armenians, even those who have left their homeland, are eager to preserve their heritage by gathering artifacts like this photo. Project SAVE/T. Hazarian

eases such as cholera and typhus, along with starvation, cut down more Armenians than Kurdish (or Turkish) bullets and bayonets.

Yet the Armenian issue refuses to go away. In the 1980's it has been incorporated into the issue of human rights in Turkey, a sore point with the United States and Turkey's European allies because of repeated evidence of serious violations of the civil and political rights of prisoners held since the 1980 military coup. Now that the country is actively seeking full membership in the European Community, there has been heavy pressure from outside on the government to meet the human rights standards observed in Western European countries.

Perhaps in response to this pressure the Turkish Foreign Minister announced in January 1989 that the Ottoman records and archives dealing with the Armenian deportations would be opened to scholars of all nations beginning in May, in an effort to resolve once and for all the question of an official Ottoman policy of Armenian genocide.

Turkey and Greece—Uneasy Partners

Despite the fact that both Turkey and Greece are NATO members and are closely allied with the United States, relations between them have been more intense and conflict ridden than those between Turkey and any other country. The Greeks were the first non-Muslim population to declare their independence from the Ottoman Empire, and Greek armies joined with those of other Balkan powers to drive the Ottomans from most of their last European territories outside of Constantinople in 1912. Conflict intensified with the Greek invasion of Anatolia after World War I. The Greek defeat left bitter memories for the Greeks, while the exchanges of the Greek population of Anatolia for the Turkish population of western Thrace caused great hardships for both communities.

Horse-drawn carts transporting coal in Erzurum. With little domestic oil, Turkey must still rely heavily on coal for fuel.   UN Photo 155438/ John Isaac

These ancient conflicts to some extent faded into the background as the threat of a Communist takeover in Greece and of Soviet aggression against Turkey brought the two countries into alignment with the United States. But beginning in the 1970's two emerging issues put them at loggerheads. The first issue was Cyprus. From the Turkish perspective, union between Cyprus and Greece might encourage Greek army leaders, who had dominated internal Greek politics since World War II, to use the island as a base for an invasion of Anatolia. Greece, for its part, angrily protested the Turkish invasion and the proclamation of a "Turkish Republic of Northern Cyprus" as a violation of international law.

Greeks and Turks

One of the interesting features of the Turkish-Greek relationship is that it is cordial and cooperative at the personal level. Greeks who live in Greek Thrace, for example, regularly cross the border to take advantage of lower prices in Edirne and other towns of Turkish Thrace, while farmers on both sides of the Meriç (Maritsa) River, which forms the border, share in a productive agriculture based on the rich Thracian soil. In the Turkish city of Edremit, local guides cheerfully point out to visitors the house at No. 8 Gozicelal Street where the father of Michael Dukakis, 1988 Democratic candidate for President of the United States, was born.

The second issue dividing Greeks and Turks involves Aegean oil exploration rights. Both Greece and Turkey are heavy oil importers and thus far have not been able to locate significant petroleum resources on their own territories. In 1970 the Greek government granted oil exploration rights to private companies in an area covering the entire eastern Aegean, and in 1974 oil was discovered there. The Turks protested that the newly discovered undersea wells were in their territorial waters, and a Turkish survey ship began drilling in the adjacent seabed. The Greeks retaliated by fortifying the offshore islands. This action led the Turks to charge that the fortifications were a violation of the Treaty of Lausanne.

Two years later, with the issue still deadlocked, oil-drilling vessels from both countries escorted by warships converged on the disputed area. The dispute was finally calmed by the U.N. Security Council, as both countries agreed to submit to international arbitration. The return of civilian government in Turkey, under a Prime Minister committed to national development led by a strong majority party, suggests that this and other issues dividing Turkey and Greece will be resolved in time. In the last couple of years the Turks have made a number of conciliatory moves, abolishing visa requirements for Greek visitors and establishing ferry services to various offshore islands. In April 1988 Prime Minister Özal met with Greek Prime Minister Papandreou in the first of a series of meetings that he said were "to shake hands and make up." Because these two leaders are realists, reconciliation seems to make more sense than continued stiff-necked dislike, especially given the instability of other countries in the eastern Mediterranean and their common need for economic development resources.

The Economy—An Uphill Climb

When the flood recedes, the mud remains.
Turkish proverb

The economy inherited by the republic from its Ottoman predecessor was meager, with few assets or prospects. Atatürk's description of conditions in Anatolia at the start of the War of Liberation aptly summed up the situation:

Our country is completely in ruins. We have not one city left that people can live in. The villages are places made of straw; it is impossible for human beings to live there. We have no roads. Our people are poor, ignorant and miserable.

Given these conditions Turkey's accomplishments in economic development have been almost miraculous. The country still lags behind Western European and other industrialized nations, but the growth of industries and exports of manufactured goods in recent years has been impressive, helping to create a middle class that lives nearly as well as do its European counterparts.

Living Standard

Per capita income, one measurement of a country's economic progress, was $1,021 annually in 1986 and $1,300 in 1988, still behind that of Greece and therefore the lowest among NATO member states. Although agriculture provides 20 percent of GNP (Gross National Product), industrial exports accounted for 71 percent of total exports in 1986 as compared with 36 percent in 1980. About 10 percent of the cars driven in Turkey today were assembled in Turkish plants, although the makes are foreign (Mercedes, General Motors, etc.).

The Ottoman Legacy

The Ottoman Empire entered the twentieth century with an undeveloped agriculture and almost no industries. The few existing industries were no more than processing plants for raw materials such as wool, cotton, raw silk, flour, and tobacco. There was little public confidence in the quality of these Ottoman products; a popular saying of the times was "If you want to hang yourself, do it with English rope." Banking, industries, mining, and foreign trade were foreign owned or controlled by non-Muslims. The few educated Muslim Turks regarded commerce and industry as beneath them, preferring careers in the armed forces or government service. As a result the republic started its existence with almost no skilled managers and little capital.

The Ottoman transportation network was as weak as the industrial structure. In 1923 there were 2,460 miles (4,100 km.) of rail track in all of Anatolia. The railroads were 100 percent foreign owned; they had

Transportation old and new.   Turkish Tourism Office

been built with European capital and technical help and were designed for shipment of raw materials to European markets or for troop transport. Paved highways were practically nonexistent on the peninsula, and at best the streets of most Turkish cities were muddy lanes. Even in Constantinople the only paved streets were on the city's European side, contrasting sharply with the refuse-strewn alleys and worn cobbled streets on the Asian side.

The republic also inherited considerable debts to foreign governments and banks from its predecessor. The Ottoman Public Debt Administration, established in 1881 by European countries to manage the empire's finances, had systematically drained off Ottoman resources through the sale of monopolies in various basic commodities (tobacco, matches, and sugar, for example) to foreigners.

A further handicap to the development of an effective functioning Ottoman economy derived from the structure of the social system. There were few hereditary landowners, nor was there a strong middle class capable of providing the money or the skills needed for economic growth. The craft guilds were well organized but lacked political power, while the self-governing towns that contributed importantly to the development of Europe were lacking in Anatolia.

Agriculture, the mainstay of the economy, was generally primitive and marked by low productivity, although some regions are fertile and productive. Most land was privately owned, held in small tracts—55 acres (25 hectares)—so that the food produced was barely sufficient for the needs of owners, leaving nothing for sale or export. In years of bad

Village women and their children in a small town south of Konya near Beyshehir.
Doranne Jacobson

Peasants

An elderly Anatolian peasant in 1909 described the conditions under which the peasants lived in the days of the empire: "Several people hold the deed for a particular field and we are not sure whether the ground we till belongs to us or not. Because of that there are fights every day and sometimes people are killed. We go to the court but we cannot explain our problem. They think only of collecting taxes when they are due. If we don't pay they take them by force, even selling our pots and bedding. Thus we are always in debt. We have had to buy seed from the *ağa* [local landowner] at either 100 to 125 *kuruş* per kilo [2.2 lbs.] or return him three kilos for one. These ağas are a menace; they can have a peasant beaten by their toughs or have him jailed."

(Irvin Schick and Ertuğrul Tonak, eds., *Turkey in Transition: New Perspectives.* New York: Oxford University Press, 1987, p. 35.)

harvests, which were frequent, farmers had no reserves and were forced to sell out or go in debt. The only people with capital were the money-lenders, who were often local notables or provincial governors who bought up large tracts from bankrupt farmers but then did nothing to improve the land.

The empire did have a well-established crafts industry, especially in fine textiles, ceramics, carpets, copper, and brassware. These various items were produced either by artisans working at home or in small shops in the bazaars of towns and cities. The bazaar today is a mainstay of the economy even if it now is less important than the factory-centered industrial system, with emphasis on exports that Turkey is developing.

The Marketplace

Istanbul's covered market (Kapalı Carşı), with its four thousand shops under one roof, is a vast crafts market. At one time it was simply a large warehouse, but as the empire's trade expanded, merchants built *hans* (inns) and roofed shops so that ships from foreign countries or arriving camel caravans could unload their cargoes and conduct business all in one place. For centuries it was the economic heart of the empire, providing employment for many artisans and earning a high reputation for their products in world markets.

Etatism, the Republican Model

Atatürk and his associates chose a state-run economy (etatism) as the logical model for development. There was an immediate practical need for government control because the rail network, the sole means of nationwide transportation, was foreign owned. Only the government had the funds needed to buy it back from its owners. But there were important psychological reasons for etatism, such as fear that foreigners would again gain control of the economy and drain off funds for development projects.

During an economic conference in Izmir in 1923 the minister of economy told the delegates: "We will not hand over Turkey, or the Turkish economy, as a country of slaves to foreign capital. . . . We are prepared to recognise . . . foreign capital, on condition that it conforms to our laws and regulations and is not granted more privileges than Turks."

Etatism, aided by loans from the Soviet Union and a small amount of aid from other countries, enabled the country to establish a number of basic industries in the 1920's. These included sugar refineries, textile plants, and cement factories. Several were privately owned; the small amount of foreign aid coming in encouraged the government to promote private investment in order to conserve its own limited funds. Turkey's oldest bank, *Iş Bankasi* (Business Bank) was founded in 1924 as a private banking institution; one of its investors was Atatürk himself, while Celal Bayar became the first general manager. But the global depression of the 1930's ended this effort at private enterprise. The trickle of foreign capital dried up and exports did not bring in enough money to pay for imports, creating chronic trade deficits.

One positive result of etatism was the establishment of a national planning system. Turkey's first Five-Year Plan was set up in 1934, and by the end of the period the country was producing a variety of consumer goods and meeting people's basic needs for clothing, housing, food, and other necessities from its own state-owned factories and processing plants. Two new government banks, Etibank and Sümerbank, were set up to help industrial development. The middle class, as well as the workers, grew rapidly in numbers and influence during World War II. These new merchants played a key role in the victory of the Democratic Party in the 1950 elections.

The Menderes government, which came to power in 1950, undertook a large-scale development program underwritten mostly by the United States. Rapid development of industries, new state banks and state economic enterprises, and an all-weather highway network seemed to indicate that Turkey was well on its way to becoming an advanced industrialized nation. The new president, Celal Bayar, declared in 1957 that the country could become a "little America" within thirty years. But the Menderes program brought problems that continue to affect the economy. They include persistent inflation, an unstable currency, uneven development of regions within the country, and heavy foreign debts.

One result of the Menderes era that had important social as well as economic consequences for the Turks was the establishment of the road network. Farmers now had direct access to town markets for their crops, and with the school following the road, villagers' horizons widened as young people began to receive an education. But the road also was an escape route for rural families, providing easy access to the city with its job opportunities and facilities. From relatively slow beginnings the migration from rural to urban areas has swelled steadily into a torrent, with 45 percent of the population living in cities as compared to 24 percent in the 1950's.

Since the 1960's several million Turks have emigrated to foreign countries—many of them directly from villages—to work, most of them going to Western Europe and, more recently, to the oil-producing countries of the Middle East. Turks living abroad are often treated poorly by their hosts, and a new set of stereotypes is emerging in Europe to replace the old image of the "fearsome Turk." But in spite of having to face prejudice and discrimination, large numbers of Turks prefer to live and work outside their home country.

Industrial Progress

Turkish industry grew rapidly in the 1950's and 1960's especially textiles and so-called heavy industry (iron and steel). British experts had helped build the first steel mill at Karabuk, on the Black Sea coast near the Pontic iron mines (which have been in operation since ancient times). The United States provided aid for a second steel mill, and a third was built in Iskenderun with Soviet help in the 1970's; the Turks played no favorites. With the completion in 1988 of three additional plants, all built by private investment, Turkish steel production should reach 9 million tons annually, making the country twenty-third in the world in total production.

The textile industry has also grown rapidly, due not only to expansion of cotton production but also to the high quality and competitive prices of Turkish finished textile goods on the world market. The industry was originally monopolized by Sümerbank, a State Economic Enterprise (SEE), but in recent years private companies have entered the field. As a result ready-to-wear clothing, bedding, linens—everything from T-shirts to elegant dresses and men's suits—labeled "Made in Turkey" are exported to Europe and now the United States through retail outlets. The popularity of Turkish ready-to-wear clothes in Western Europe in recent years prompted the European Economic Community (EEC) to set import quotas in order to protect its own manufacturers; Turkish exporters were undercutting them because of lower labor costs and easier access to raw materials.

A Shaky Economy

Despite these encouraging developments the Turkish economy continues to struggle against handicaps that have not been easy to overcome. The major handicap was and is inflation, which runs in cycles but generally has undermined economic gains. Various forces have contributed to the inflation spiral: artifically high farm subsidies, government support for basic necessities (bread, cooking oil, sugar, salt) to keep prices within reach of the poor, and the cost of maintaining the second-largest army in NATO, to name a few.

By 1980 inflation was averaging more than 100 percent a year, and foreign investors were increasingly reluctant to put money into a country wracked by civil war. Labor strikes and walkouts cost more in lost work hours, with the resulting drop in production, than they had in the previous six years. The four-fold jump in world oil prices after 1973 had been another blow; Turkey has almost no petroleum resources and must import over 80 percent of its oil. Remittances (money sent home) from Turkish workers abroad were down by 60 percent from pre-1974 levels. The balance-of-payments deficit (the difference between what a country earns from exports and what it must spend for imported goods) had reached $3.1 billion, and interest payments on foreign debts siphoned off funds urgently needed for oil imports and equipment for the completion of important development projects.

The military coup of 1980 was carried out not only because of the failure of the major political parties to control civil violence and cooperate for effective government, but also because of their inability to manage the economy. The International Monetary Fund (IMF), Turkey's principal creditor, had been warning the country for some time to put its economic house in order as a prerequisite for further loans and delaying of interest payments due on its foreign debts. Immediately following the coup the military leaders introduced an economic stabilization program intended to curb inflation and meet IMF requirements. The administrator of the program was Turgut Özal, the economist turned politician who became Prime Minister with the restoration of civilian government and is now in his second term in office.

One of Özal's political opponents once described him as a "mosaicist, a man who believes that if you put all the pieces in right, you will end up with a picture." Özal's prescription for the economy is simple: Free it from etatism and force it to compete. To accomplish this goal, a major effort has been undertaken to reduce state control of the economy and encourage private investment. In 1980 some three thousand state-managed development projects were abruptly canceled, although most of them were already underway. A number of State Economic Enterprises (SEEs) that have controlled metal industries, aircraft manufacturing, machine tools, textiles, animal foodstuffs, and many others since etatism began were disbanded. Others were reorganized for greater efficiency; good managers were rewarded with promotions and pay increases, while mediocre ones or those unwilling to adapt to the new policies were shuffled off to the dark corners of public service.

Prospects

As the decade of the 1980's nears its end, Turkey is a busy place, humming with activity like the hive of the honeybee that serves as the symbol of the Motherland Party. The Özal government believes it can reshape the economy to make the country an advanced industrialized state in twenty years. It is a bold vision. Whether the country will continue to support Özal's admittedly painful economic restrictions is not yet clear. Well-intentioned efforts by previous prime ministers in the 1960's and 1970's to introduce strict austerity measures met strong political opposition. Although the Motherland Party still holds a majority in the National Assembly, its popular support has dropped since Özal's reelection.

Turkey has a number of economic assets to balance its weaknesses. It provides a variety of crops that can be sold to other countries. A failure or decline in production of one crop can be offset by increased exports in another, and the variations in regional climate and soils ensure agricultural diversity. The country has a large skilled labor force, which enables Turkish firms to compete successfully for foreign contracts, especially in construction projects, as their wage levels are lower than those of many other industrial countries.

Under the Özal government Turkey courts foreign investors. Agribusiness, textiles, processed foods, and other industries have begun to grow rapidly and to attract investors. If Turkey becomes a full member of the European Economic Community, its economy will probably continue to prosper.

From Village to City

The peasant is the master of the country.
Atatürk

Turkey today is in a state of transition from a land of small, compact, long-established villages to one of vast cities, which have become almost unmanageable as more and more villagers crowd in from the country-side. The consequences of this transition, particularly its effect on Turkish society, are far from clear, but it is a clear break with the past.

Although cities have existed for several thousand years in Anatolia, people gathered mainly in villages or small market towns. The rise and fall of cities over many centuries hardly affected town and village life until well into the twentieth century.

Most of these villages and towns were built on far earlier foundations. As was noted earlier in this book, many different peoples migrated into Anatolia over the centuries, and as a result a mosaic pattern of settlement was established with people generally settling near their relatives. For example, Armenians were found primarily in eastern Anatolia, while Greek-speaking peoples settled along the Aegean. The reasons for

these various settlement patterns are not clear, but with the migration of Turkish peoples into Anatolia, communal village organization took on a form that has been preserved until the present day. Being semi-nomads and stock raisers, the early Turks had three requirements for a place in which they would settle: It had to have a dependable water supply, protection from surprise attack, and sufficient pasturage for their flocks.

Two common types of villages (*köy,* in Turkish), the escarpment and the river-valley *köy,* met these requirements. Escarpment villages are found either on high ground such as a mesa or tableland, or dug into hillsides overlooking the pastureland. The river-valley *köy* is a common sight from highways that pass near the great Anatolian rivers—a huddle of mud-brick houses overtopped by the minaret of the local mosque and half hidden among the poplars and willows that mark its water supply.

Migration under the Ottomans

As their empire expanded, Ottoman rulers encouraged Turkish tribes living outside their borders to move into Anatolia, in a deliberate policy intended to provide a steady supply of warriors for their armies and ensure a loyal population. Meanwhile, non-Muslim villages were left largely undisturbed under the *millet* system of grouping such peoples on the basis of religious identification for administrative purposes. Other than the visits of officials to collect the poll tax on Christians and of recruitment officers from the Janissary corps, these villages remained isolated from urban and imperial Ottoman life.

Muslim villages in Anatolia had much the same experience. There was hardly any migration from village to village and little incentive to

A winding cobbled street in Göreme. Many country towns still have streets like this.
Joseph Lawton

· 165 ·

move to the cities for most villagers in Ottoman times. As a result village populations were mostly interrelated, having sprung from the original settler families. Often lands and entire villages were granted to Ottoman officers in return for heroic service in war. The villagers farmed them but were allowed to keep only enough of the crop to live on; the rest went to the owner, the tax collector, and local officials. The Sultan's government provided rough justice in the person of the *kadi* (religious judge), but little else. To the outsider or city resident village life seemed characterized by isolation, poverty, and ignorance.

Yet for the villagers this admittedly harsh existence had its compensations. Their lives were shaped by the agricultural calendar, with its rhythm of the seasons, in a cycle of sowing, harvesting, and reaping, interspersed with births, circumcisions, weddings, and deaths. In Muslim villages special events connected with Islam—such as the festival of Şeker Bayrami, which marks the end of the fasting month of Ramazan—were highlights of the year. Families were close knit, with few differences of wealth or class and maximum security for family members including the elderly. Most villages were self-sufficient in food production, and there was usually a surplus that farmers could bring to the weekly market in nearby towns and barter for the few necessities they could not provide for themselves.

Due to the multi-ethnic, multireligious nature of the empire, Muslims and non-Muslims lived, worked, and worshiped side by side, enriching and strengthening their separate cultures but seldom mixing. There was considerable tolerance between them despite unequal social positions and the Ottoman Islamic view of non-Muslims as inferior peoples. But neither at the village level nor in cities did the sort of ethnically mixed neighborhoods develop that have become a feature of American society. Separation of peoples even extended to a division of labor along ethnic lines.

An English consul's report on Black Sea villages in the 1860's noted that Turks were usually found as sailors, fishermen, and carpenters; Kurds were shepherds; Greeks were apt to be stonecutters and shopkeepers; while the Armenians followed the trades of shoemaking, tailoring, and jewelry making.

Changing Villages

Village life began to change slowly with the establishment of the republic. Villages were given legal status for the first time in 1924 under a village law that provided for an elected headman *(muhtar)* and an elected council of elders legally empowered to collect taxes, mediate disputes, and undertake development projects.

There are today about 35,000 villages in Turkey, comprising 50 percent of the population. Thirty years ago the rural–urban ratio was 70 percent to 30 percent; in the 1970's it was 60–40 percent. Almost certainly by the year 2000 there will be more urban residents than villagers. Yet even then the majority of the population will still be one generation or less removed from the village. Many transplanted villagers remain ambivalent about their rural past.

The changes in lifestyle accelerated after 1950 are due largely to the development of the two-party system. In its effort to win the elections the Democratic Party took its campaign directly to the rural people. Suddenly candidates for the National Assembly appeared in villages. The reaction of people in the writer Mahmut Makal's village to one such visit is probably typical:

A stream of candidates descended on the village. No sooner had one taxi or jeep driven off than two others arrived, with flags on their hoods. The visitors got up on a stone block with reams of paper in their hands and read interminably. It's as though there were no end to our troubles. Party lists and ballots

In the Village

Aziz Nesin, in his *Autobiography*, describes his father's village:
"The people of Gölve are sound, strong, enduring, honest and
bound to their home. They can't really leave this place and their
sterile, unfit land. The boys leave home at an early age and go to
Istanbul in order to work and make money. What they earn they
send to the village. No matter what they do, they will finally return
to Gölve; when they die they will be buried in the barren, treeless,
unproductive, neglected soil of Gölve."

are confusing, especially to the women, although the men know by the mark
on it to which party a list belongs. Oh dear, a new fellow has turned up who
calls himself a Democrat. We're recording our votes for him; they say he'll
make everything cheaper. What name is it? This one or that? (Mahmut Makal,
Bizim Köy [*Our Village*], published in English as *A Village in Anatolia*.
London: Valentine Mitchell, 1954, pp. 139–41.)

The rural vote made the difference in the 1950 elections. Although
most voters could do no better than mark an "X" on their ballots, the
results swept the Democrats into office.

Rural-Urban Migration

Elections brought new ideas to the countryside; new roads, many built
by officials who wanted to keep the rural vote, had a more dramatic
effect: a massive movement of villagers to the cities. There are a number
of reasons for this large-scale flight of unskilled workers into the cities.
These internal immigrants can not only earn more money in the cities,

but also gain social status in the eyes of those who remain in the village. Workers who have learned some skills move from factory to factory and project to project, somewhat like construction workers in the United States; while others move to the city to take advantage of greater educational opportunities there.

The "Squatter Settlements"

An urban problem, which is, however, a link between rural emigrants and the villages they left behind, is that of squatter settlements, low-income urban slums. In Turkey they are called *gecekondu*, meaning literally "put up overnight." Under Turkish customary law anyone who builds a house or other building overnight on unoccupied municipal

Gecekondu settlement in Ankara. UN Photo 155429/ John Isaac

land, completing it with four walls, floor, and roof by morning, cannot be evicted except through a lengthy legal process. For both urban and rural low-income groups the practice has meant economic salvation. As early as 1969, 65 percent of the population of Ankara lived in *gecekondu*s. The percentage is far higher now. For most visitors their first sight of the capital is row upon row of tiny houses spread over the hillsides like barnacles on a tidal rock. Yet these structures that started out as simple huts of tin sheeting, scavenged bricks, and old lumber have gradually evolved into permanent houses with city water and sewage, electricity, refrigerators, even TV. The *gecekondu*s serve an important function in modern Turkish society. They are, in a sense, Anatolian villages transplanted to the city.

However, even in these low-income settlements the social gap between residents and their village relatives is widening. A *gecekondu* resident spoke of his father:

Now and then he came from the village to visit us. I, his son, wore a light, cool nylon shirt while he, my father, was suffocating in homemade coarse cloth. He wore rubber shoes which froze his feet in winter and cooked them in summer, while I wore comfortable leather shoes. My father's clothes were old and dirty, and I was apprehensive to walk around with him. I was in fact afraid that someone might ask who he was. The differences between us were so great that I could not say that he was my father." (Quoted in Kemal Karpat, *The Gecekondu: Rural Migration and Urbanization.* Cambridge, England: Cambridge University Press, 1976, p. 161.)

Those Who Remain

Despite the numerous temptations of the city for Anatolian villagers, there are many areas of the country where village life remains strong. As more social services are brought to the villages, the rate of rural-to-urban migration can be expected to slacken. The present government has undertaken a major effort to discourage urban migration by developing the poorer areas of the country. The Southeastern Anatolia Project (SAP), a network of dams and irrigation tunnels now under way in the arid underdeveloped southeast, is expected to change the lives of nearly 5 million people in six provinces, most of them different ethnically from the Turkish majority. The contrast between what has become possible for these people, largely Kurds, in the future and their recent past is graphically illustrated in Orhan Kemal's short story about Kurdish villagers written in 1961:

> . . . Farm hands, fifteen or twenty in a row, worked steadily at the weeds around the seedlings. The temperature soared to a hundred and forty-nine in the sun. No bird flew in the shimmering, dust-gray sky. . . . Ferho Üzeyir wiped the sweat off his swollen hands on his baggy black trousers and turned his bloodshot eyes on his wife swinging her hoe beside him. . . . He spoke in Kurdish, "Whatsa matter?"
>
> Gulizar gave her husband a weary glance. Her eyes had sunk with fright into their sockets. Her hoe suddenly slipped from her hand to the ground. Pressing her huge belly with her hands, she bent over, then fell to her knees on the red earth everywhere cracked by the blistering sun. ("Baby Born in the Field," in Leo Hamalian, ed., *New Writing from the Middle East.* New York: New American Library, 1978, p. 421.)

Urban Change

In the last years of the Ottoman Empire a journalist predicted what he thought would happen when the Turks threw in their lot with Europe: "There is no second civilization. Civilization means European civilization and it must be imported with both its roses and its thorns." Since Atatürk's time Turkey has been adopting more and more features of European and American civilization, roses as well as thorns. As more people crowd into the cities, the demands for housing, clean water, medical services, education, and other needs increase beyond the capacity of either government or private investors to meet them. Thus about 350,000 housing units a year are needed for new city residents, most of them low-income people, but the government has thus far been able to budget funds for only 175,000.

The wholesale importation of contemporary architecture has also begun to take effect on Turkish cities. While villagers fresh from the country tend to regard the multistory concrete-block buildings that become their new homes as improvements on their rural houses, much of the comfort and ease of Anatolian rural life has been lost. Mammoth projects replace buildings designed for families. This loss of scale even affects efforts by city governments to improve livability by developing parks and better transportation. The mayor of Istanbul recently ordered a block of small workshops on the Golden Horn to be bulldozed and replaced by a waterside park and superhighway. The action not only eliminated a large number of jobs but also removed a colorful though shabby area of the city that had existed for centuries.

What is developing in Turkish society, as a result of the importation of ideas about city life first developed in cities such as New York and Paris, is a two-class structure. At the top is a "European-style" middle class that is becoming more and more separated from the lower class of *gecekondu* dwellers, manual laborers, and villagers. Many members of this class are well dressed and are educated abroad. They are often fluent in several languages and trained in the latest European or American types of management and scientific research. The challenge for Turkey is how to bring these classes more into balance, preserving the qualities that give traditional society its cohesion and strength while continuing to develop educational and economic services that will enable this population to realize its potential and live with a sense of dignity and self-worth.

A shoeshine man in Istanbul. The design of his stand is traditional, but the faces on the front are not.   Maury Englander

Women in the Society

One important measurement of the strength and progressiveness of a society is the role of its women. In traditional Muslim village society women had, and generally still have, a central role in child rearing and the organization of family life. But it is largely a subservient role. Village elders are usually male, and women take little part in village leadership. Women are often expected to obey father, grandfather, and eventually husband and son (although the obligation becomes reciprocal with the son's responsibility to care for his aged mother). When visitors arrive at a Muslim village home, the only woman permitted into the

Women making gözleme, a crepelike bread in a village in the Taurus Mountains. Gözleme is often served wrapped around cheese or chopped meat.   Maury Englander

misafir odası (literally, "guest room," the main room where guests are received) would be the husband's mother.

A similar division of labor and responsibility existed in non-Muslim communities. For example, in Armenian villages in eastern Anatolia each of the small adobe or stone houses sheltered an extended family whose oldest male was the head of the house. Women held the same subordinate roles as their Muslim counterparts. Men did not interfere in the work of women and vice versa.

In the work area there are fewer distinctions. Women work in the fields alongside men, and at harvesttime whole families share in the harvesting process. The mechanization of Turkish agriculture since 1950, however, has eased the burden of work for both men and women. But village women's roles have not changed greatly, although even there the winds of change are blowing.

Atatürk was a strong believer in the rights and responsibilities of women to "contribute to the general effort to improve the happiness and well-being of our society." He established a committee in 1923 to review and reform Islamic family law. Polygamy was made illegal, equality was granted to women in divorce proceedings, and there was considerable freedom in dress. The educational level among women is rising, and successful efforts have been made to bring urban women into the mainstream of the work force. Many women serve in the professions and, as senior officials in the government, and there are women judges. However, there are few women in politics either at the Assembly level or in top positions in political parties, and there are few signs that this will change in the near future.

Education and Youth

Education has been a priority in Turkey since the start of the republic. With almost 100 percent illiteracy in rural areas and very few schools, the job of educating a population spread over a huge territory was monumental. Atatürk began by setting up teacher-training institutes throughout the country and introduced a program of rural education and basic literacy for adults through Village Institutes. (These have now become regular primary schools.) At the start of independence there was one university, in Istanbul; now there are eighteen, with at least one in each region to serve regional needs. The results of this effort have been impressive. The literacy rate, although still higher for men than women and low in areas such as eastern Anatolia, is now 72 percent; in 1960 it was 40 percent.

Although education is considered the key to professional advancement and upward mobility, educational facilities have not kept pace with population growth. This fact puts a severe strain on society, and particularly on youth. Some 50 percent of the population is under the age of twenty. With facilities limited there is intense competition; thus in 1987 over four thousand primary-school students took entrance examinations for three hundred places in the ninth-grade class at the prestigious Galatasaray Lise (a combination high school and junior college), which prepares the country's best students for higher education. Competition at the university level is equally keen. Turkish families often make great sacrifices for their children's education, believing with considerable justification that it is a means whereby poverty or low social status can be overcome.

However, as Turkey moves into the last decade of the twentieth century, the goal of a population of youth educated at least through the elementary grades, and preferably trained in vocational skills, may well become a casualty of the country's economic problems. With the inflation rate averaging 75 percent a year and factory workers earning about $125 per month, children have become more valuable to many families as economic providers than as students. "I was going to school but [my family] thought it was better for me to learn how to earn money," says a twelve-year-old boy from eastern Turkey who was sent to Istanbul in 1986 to learn a trade; he carries tubes to workmen in a car repair shop. Other youngsters hunch over sewing machines in an attic, piecing out men's ties, or shine shoes on the sidewalks of city streets. Textile plants in particular often hire children in preference to adults, because the overcrowded school system allows them to drop out and they can work long hours at less pay, with no health insurance or other benefits that must be paid to adult workers.

Graduates of such elite schools as Bosporus University (formerly Robert College) or Middle East Technical University in Ankara automatically become part of a network of contacts valuable throughout life. An American writer noted education's social importance three decades ago: "Children of the rich and poor, children of cabinet ministers and of gatekeepers are classmates in the schools."

(Eleanor Bisbee, *The Young Turks.* Philadelphia: University of Pennsylvania Press, 1951, p. 87.)

The country is fortunate also in not having a generation gap between leaders and youth. Most business and government leaders are in their forties, including Prime Minister Özal and his cabinet. This provides government and people with a shared dynamism. Turkish young people outwardly are not vastly different from their counterparts throughout the world. They tend to dress casually, the prevailing style being faded denims and tennis shoes. The continued emphasis on strong family ties and respect for elders and teachers tends to make them somewhat less apt to oppose or disagree with their parents than was the case in the 1970's when so many young Turks were drawn to terrorism. But they are a lively lot, in their school-yard basketball games or debating forums. One suspects they could step into the shoes of their grand-fathers who smuggled weapons through the streets of Istanbul to Atatürk's beleaguered army sixty years ago. Turkish youth will shortly have the country's future in their hands. It is a future built upon an ancient past, marked by great ages and equally great collapses, and by many false starts. But the progress visible in less than a decade of a new start augurs well for Turkey in the next century.

Aspects of Turkish Culture

Epochs seem hidden in seeds,
Swings creaking in the soil.
Melih Cevdet Anday, *On the Nomad Sea*

The soil of Anatolia has nourished many civilizations over the centuries. Each of these civilizations developed over time a particular way of life, which may best be described as their *culture.* The anthropologist Ruth Benedict, in her book *Patterns of Culture*, notes that "from the moment of his birth the customs into which [an individual] is born shape his experience and behavior. By the time he can talk, he is the little creature of his culture." The Turks, relative latecomers to Anatolia, also developed over time their particular culture, blended from many influences. They were early on a part of the larger Islamic society, then a multiethnic empire, and now a modern nation. Turkish boys and girls today are surrounded both by the past and by a set of cultural influences from abroad, images of European, American and other cultures. But such cultural elements as architecture, handicrafts, language, literature and customs, even cooking, continue to provide identification for them as members of a particular society.

Architecture

Architecture has been an important feature of many great civilizations in Turkey, from the Greek and Roman to Byzantine, Islamic, and European. The Ottoman emphasis on "grand architecture" in buildings suited to their imperial power has endowed modern Turkey with mosques, palaces, and other structures of great beauty and high quality in design and workmanship. The architect synonymous with this "grand style," Mimar Sinan, began his career as a military engineer in the Janissaries, and the structures associated with him are notable for their imaginative application of engineering principles. The minarets of his masterpiece, the Selimiye mosque in Edirne, soar over two hundred feet into the Thracian sky.

The "Blue Mosque" of Sultan Ahmet I (1603–1617) in Istanbul was built to be the finest such structure in the Islamic world. The architect provided it with six minarets, which became an embarrassment since the Great Mosque in Mecca also had six. A seventh minaret was hastily added to the Great Mosque so that the Sultan could not be accused of impropriety!

Today boys and girls in Turkish cities and towns live, study, and worship surrounded by a particular architectural atmosphere. The skyline of Istanbul conveys this atmosphere, as does the Galatasaray Lise (high school), where students attend classes in buildings converted from a medieval *bedesten* (covered market). On the return from school these same students often pass ancient cemeteries; their long-dead occupants lie under gravestones tilted at crazy angles, surmounted by turbans and inscribed with long Koranic verses. The neighborhood mosque with its tall, metal-sheathed minaret, the *hammams* (public baths, many of them built by great Ottoman architects such as Sinan), and other structures help to reinforce this sense of belonging to a unique society.

Modern Turkish architects have generally remained faithful to their predecessors in design, while employing new methods in construction technology. Three Turkish buildings won first prizes in the first Aga Khan competition for structures that best combine modern technology with historic-preservation techniques in the Islamic world. One, the Rustem Paşa caravanserai in Edirne, was a sixteenth-century hostelry that had fallen into disuse; it has been restored and modernized as a hotel. The new building of the Turkish Historical Society in Ankara, completely modern in style and facilities, conveys the sense of a medieval library and *medrese* (Islamic religious upper school), which was its function.

The third prize winner was a private home in Bodrum, a south Aegean port encircled by hills fragrant with olive, lime, and lemon trees and sheltered behind a crescent-shaped harbor. In the nineteenth century wealthy Turks began to build *konaks*, summer seaside homes of whitewashed masonry from the rough-hewn, heavily mortared native stone, in Bodrum and other coastal towns. Architect Turgut Cansever and a local carpenter brought two adjoining *konaks* together into a single dwelling, rescued the ancient walled garden from years of neglect, and integrated the former *selamlik* (men's quarters) and *haremlik* (women's quarters) into modern space so well that the house has become a model of restoration for the town.

Bodrum, ancient Halicarnassus, was the site of the fourth-century B.C. mausoleum of King Mausolus, and was one of the Seven Wonders of the ancient world.

Art and Literature

With certain exceptions Turkish art and literature today fit into the artistic and literary styles of the modern world. Such Turkish artists as

Rahmi Pehlivanli, "the painter of kings," concentrate on portraits of rulers and statesmen and large landscapes of provinces or regions, which are intended, as he says himself, to transport and promote people of various parts of Turkey to each other. Other Turkish painters past and present have tended toward the derivative rather than the original. Thus Ottoman court painters worked to win the favor and support of wealthy patrons, who would provide them with the best materials plus an army of apprentices to run their errands.

One of the paintings of Osman Hamdi (1842–1910) depicts an elaborate dinner party in a garden filled with tulips (which originated in the Ottoman empire and were brought to Holland in the sixteenth century by a returning traveler.) In the painting musicians playing flutes and small drums circulate among the guests, along with huge turtles carrying lighted candelabra on their shells.

One area of originality in Turkish art is that of the miniature painting. Miniature paintings probably began in Islamic Iran, but they attained high levels of perfection under the Ottomans. When European travelers began visiting Ottoman lands regularly in the eighteenth and nineteenth centuries, they recorded their observations in diaries and journals. Since they lacked photographic equipment needed to make a permanent record of their visits, they made much use of the "bazaar painters," itinerant artists who would make rapid miniature on-the-spot drawings of bazaar and street scenes, much as a street-corner artist in Europe or the United States will sketch one's portrait or do a group sketch of a visiting family at fairs or tourist centers. These miniatures are noted for economy of scene, and for detailed and accurate pictorial images, and they provide important visual information on what life was like in Turkey at the time.

Modern Turkish writers also use familiar forms of expression—

poetry, novels, plays, and short stories—to develop their themes. Some of them, such as the poet Nazim Hikmet, were strongly influenced by Marxism and emphasized social justice (or injustice) in their work. But Hikmet and his contemporaries also draw effective word pictures of Turkish society during the last days of the empire and the transition to the republic.

The leading Turkish novelists also tend toward social criticism in their works. The outstanding example is Mahmut Makal's *Bizim Köy (Our Village)*, published in 1950 and based on the author's experiences in a remote, poverty-stricken Anatolian village. Both Yashar Kemal and Orhan Kemal (no relation), whose works have been quoted elsewhere in this book, have suffered censorship or sometimes imprisonment for their depiction of social problems in their work, while Aziz Nesin, the country's leading satirist, spent a good part of his life behind bars.

Magic Carpets

Turkish carpets, including the flat-woven mats called *kilims*, are the best-known handicraft product and an important export item. Long before European furniture became popular in Turkey, families were accustomed to recline on pillows or low cushioned sofas called divans in the rooms of their homes; the floors, usually of tile, were covered with fine carpets. These carpets had been woven by village women and dyed with natural vegetable dyes. The carpet industry is still concentrated in village homes or small weaving sheds "out back," and although chemical or chrome dyes are popular, the majority of the weavers seem to prefer the natural ones.

An American visitor who queried villagers as to their dye preferences was given equivocal answers; his host suggested that they might be more con-

There are many different designs of carpets in Turkey. Some are identified with a particular town or region, such as the Bergama design produced by weavers in Manisa, or the Azeri carpets of northeastern Anatolia. The cities of Isparta and Kayseri have their own special designs, while the Hereke style woven throughout the country has come down to the present little changed from Ottoman days.

Weaving is an important income-producing activity in many villages. Compared to the huge carpet factories in the United States and elsewhere, the industry is small-scale. It takes little capital; a father buys a loom or two, and a stock of yarn, and puts his wife and daughters to work in a family enterprise. The girls come home after school and immediately go to work on the loom, the older ones weaving, the younger ones spinning wool. Some weavers use graph-paper cartoons for their designs, with only the overall pattern of carpets from their particular area to guide them. But more often the weaver is on her own, creating a design that springs from her imagination, an artist whose work unfolds slowly as she weaves. Village weavers often develop a proprietary feeling for a carpet even if it has been commissioned for sale, and are unwilling to part with it when it is finished.

Other Crafts Specialties

Despite the inroads of machine-made products and imports from Japan, the United States, and Western Europe, Turkey still has a thriving

The Dowry

An American buyer tells of a carpet he had commissioned from a weaver; when it was finished she refused to sell it to him: She wished to save it for her *çeyik* (dowry). The carpet featured a design of cranes flying, with a border of colored rosettes. Cranes bring good luck in Turkey, as in many countries; and the weaver, upon looking at the finished product, decided that she needed to start her marriage under favorable circumstances, promising the buyer "one just like it" to ease her conscience and keep faith.

handicrafts industry, and places like the Grand Bazaar in Istanbul still have their tiny shops turning out handmade brassware, copper, pottery, and leather goods. The pastel blue and green Kütahya ware made in the city of that name was described earlier in this book; most Turkish tile and ceramic making is done there, although the blue Iznik tiles that were a major element in mosque decoration for centuries have been revived in recent years on a small scale in that ancient city. Turkish copper is another important craft specialty; master coppersmiths are artists in making *new* copper trays, pots, pans, etc. that can hardly be distinguished from centuries-old ones.

A traveler tells of a visit to a master coppersmith in his closet-sized shop outside the Grand Bazaar. "See that old copper waterpipe?" asked the smith. "It dates from the time of Ahmet III [1703–1730] and was used by the Sultan himself. I just finished making it yesterday." (Tom Brosna-han, Turkey: A Travel Survival Kit. *Victoria, Australia.: Lonely Planet Publications, 1985, p. 62.)*

Turkish Cuisine

Turkey shares with its eastern Mediterranean neighbors a love of food and the art of cooking. A Turkish proverb says "Choose your friends by the taste of their food," and the greatest compliment one can pay to a cook for an outstanding meal or dish is to say *"Elinize sağlık,"* "Long live your hands." When sitting down to eat, the host's usual "blessing" is *"afiyet olsun,"* "May this be good for your health."

Turkish cuisine is part of the larger cookery of the eastern Mediterranean, with similar ingredients and many of the same dishes. Throughout this region stuffed eggplants, tomatoes, bell peppers, zucchini, and rice are common features on dinner tables, while the smell of roast lamb and mutton cooking over charcoal hangs in the air. The Turkish horsemen brought their art of grilling meat on spits or skewers over a huge campfire after they had pitched their tents at the end of a day on horseback. They may also have brought yogurt, since it is an indispensable element in Turkish cooking along with garlic and olive oil. Yogurt is used in soups, stews, sauces, and even salads. Vegetables cooked in olive oil, peppers, eggplant, peas, beans, are another mainstay of the Turkish diet, and extensive use of olive oil is traditionally said to guarantee a long life.

As is the case throughout the eastern Mediterranean area, rice usually accompanies all meat dishes. It is referred to as rice *pilaf* (or pilav or pilau, depending on one's language) which means simply "cooked through." The original Turkish contribution of skewered meats has become universally known as *kebab*, meaning literally "roasted meat." *Şiş kebab* (meat roasted on a skewer interspersed with tomato chunks, pieces of onion, and peppers) is the commonest form of kebab. *Döner kebab,* which is the nearest thing to a Turkish national dish, is lamb roasted on a vertical turning spit until it forms a thick crust; the crust is then cut off with a huge knife and the roasting continues,

A fish seller plying his trade beside the Galata Bridge in Istanbul.   Joseph Lawton

with thin strips cut off as it cooks.

This brief account of Turkish cuisine would not be complete without mention of some of its settings and the special experience of "dining out" in the country. In cities a meal at a small *ocakbaşı kebapçi* ("fireside kebab café") is one such experience. Patrons sit around a long rectangular firepit, with the master *kebapçi* in the middle like a Japanese chef, working like a demon as he grills skewers of lamb, *köfte* (meatballs), *çöp kebab* (morsels of lamb on split bamboo skewers), and other meat dishes to order.

In the villages dining etiquette is more elaborate, at least when visitors are present. Villagers say that the hungry person is *tanrı misafırı* ("a guest sent by God to be welcomed with hospitality"), and they go all out in their welcome. The visitor is ushered into the *misafır odası* ("social room" or guest room) and seated on carpets and pillows around a low table. Course after course appears magically from a tiny kitchen somewhere out back. There are *mezeler*, Turkish "appetizers," such as *böreks*, cylinders of phyllo dough filled with white cheese and parsley; *dolma*, stuffed vine leaves; perhaps a dish of stuffed eggplant called *imam bayıldı* ("the imam fainted," supposedly because the sight of this dish was too much for the first religious leader to be presented with it). There may be a yogurt soup or one called *yayla* ("summer pasture"), local mushrooms gathered that very morning by the villagers, and a pot-cooked stew accented with parsley, dill, nutmeg, or cinnamon, as a main dish, garnished with rice and homemade noodles. No one goes away hungry from a Turkish meal, whether it is in a village home, a fish restaurant by the Bosporus, or a tiny *döner kebab* stand tucked away on a city side street.

Popular Literature

It is a common observation that Turks are a serious people by nature, grave and decorous in their behavior. The Danish storyteller Hans Christian Andersen visited Constantinople in 1841 and referred to Turkish gravity in his journal:

A gondola flew by, rich and swift, and in the stern, on high colored cushions and fine carpets, sat a grave Turk, his arms crossed. . . .

[in the Bazaar] . . . The Turk sits, serious and grave, with his long pipe in his mouth; the Jew and the Greek are busy, they shout and wave. The motley human throng masses its way through the criss-cross arches, and through it rides, very gravely, a distinguished Turk, who looks neither to right nor left." (*A Poet's Bazaar.* Translated by Grace Thornton. New York: Michael Kesend, 1988, p. 130, p. 105.)

But there is another side to Turkish gravity, a rich lode of humor often laced with satire and expressed in folk tales and popular drama that have come down to the modern Turks little changed in form or content. Turkish folktales range from less than a minute to twenty or thirty hours in length, the longer ones often being reserved to tell during the long nights of the Ramazan month of fasting. The tales have many heroes, including Koroğlu (Son of the Blind Man), a Turkish Robin Hood.

The major folk hero in Turkish literature, and the national funny-man, is Nasrettin Hoca. Little is known about his life, but he was apparently a real person, a *hoca* (schoolteacher) in the small city of Akşehir. When he was a small boy, he and his classmates planned to play a trick on their teacher. They were caught red-handed, and each boy was punished according to his part in the plan. Nasrettin had been told to watch and laugh when the trick was played, so his teacher imposed the perfect punishment: "Let people laugh at you, as long as there are people in the world capable of laughter!"

Turks have been laughing at Hoca and his droll stories for nearly six hundred years now without letup. There is practically no situation in daily life that does not have a Hoca story to fit its circumstances or point a moral lesson. They often begin with the phrase "One day the Hoca," which is enough to double up a Turk with amusement. Two typical Hoca stories appear on the next page.

As the stories show, Hoca was wise and devout, but he had the foibles and weaknesses common to all humans. In true Turkish tradition he remains hospitable, warm, amusing, and lovable. His tomb in Akşehir has a tall iron fence in front of it with a gate locked by a huge padlock. But behind the tomb there is nothing: To visit it one has only to walk around the fence.

Uniquely Turkish also is the cycle of shadow-puppet plays called *Karagöz*, after the name of their leading character. The origins of these plays spring from far back in the Turkish past, in early Ottoman times. As the story goes, the great Sultan Orkhan had hired a crew of workmen to build a mosque in Bursa, his new capital. The foreman of the crew

Once the Hoca . . .

One hot day the Hoca was resting in the shade of a walnut tree between chores in his garden. After a time he began to notice the huge watermelons growing on vines in a nearby field, and the walnuts in the tree over his head. "Sometimes I can't understand the ways of Allah," he mused. "Look at that great watermelon growing on such a spindly vine, and those tiny walnuts growing on that lordly tree. If I had been the Creator, I should have put the walnut on the vine and the watermelon on the tree."

Just then a walnut fell from the tree and landed smack on the Hoca's head. Rubbing the lump, he looked up toward the sky and said: "Forgive me, Allah, for questioning your wisdom. You are all-wise. Where would I be now if watermelons grew on trees?"

The Chief Judge of Akşehir was a notoriously avaricious man and accordingly was disliked by the Hoca. One day the Judge asked the Hoca to find him a good greyhound in time for the hunting season.

A few days later the Hoca arrived at the city court bringing a well-fed sheepdog as large as a medium-sized donkey. On seeing the dog, the Judge was convinced that the Hoca was an ignorant fool. "Can't you tell the difference between a greyhound and this beast?" he asked. "Even a child would not confuse this creature with a greyhound, which is the leanest animal alive!"

"I can't see any reason for you to be upset, Your Honor," replied the Hoca. "I can guarantee that after a few weeks with you, this poor dog will be leaner than the leanest hound!"

was one Hacıvad, and one of the principal workmen was Karagöz ("Black Eyes" in Turkish). They were both funny men, and their conversation on the job was so amusing that the other workmen stopped to laugh. Work on the mosque went slower and slower, and finally stopped entirely because the workmen were laughing so hard. The Sultan became very angry, and ordered both men hanged. Some accounts say that this was done during a festival and that there was a great public outcry, which caused Orhan to regret his action. Other accounts say that their heads were cut off and Karagöz and Hacıvad carried their heads under their arms to complain to the Sultan. Whatever the facts, the ruler came to feel that he had made a mistake, especially when a friend of the two funnymen, a leatherworker, told him some of their anecdotes. The Sultan ordered the leatherworker to cut out leather figures of Karagöz and Hacıvad, manipulating them behind a screen so that people would think they were still alive. In this way Karagöz and Hacıvad became shadow puppets, surrounded by a galaxy of other characters. The *Karagöz* puppet shows were especially popular in villages; the puppets could satirize the authorities without being punished, and villagers roared with laughter at the outwitting of the rapacious tax collector or the cruel governor.

Today the art of *Karagöz* is dying out. It takes years of training and a great variety of skills besides simple mastery of puppet technique. There are over two hundred characters in the plays, each one made from a piece of hide that must be cleaned, scraped with glass until it is translucent, and tanned until all the hairs can be removed. Then the pattern for the figure is incised on the hide and cut out with special knives, and the outline pierced with a curved blade so that light can pass through it. Finally the figure is painted with translucent madder dyes characteristic of Ottoman times. The contours of each figure are edged with black so that they can be seen better on the screen, and all the pieces are sewn together at the joints.

Karagöz *puppets.*   Reprinted from *Turk Golge Oyunu*, by Nureddin Sevin, © Devlet Kitaplari, Istanbul, 1968.

All of this work takes many hours, as does developing the dexterity required to manipulate the puppets; as a result, few apprentices are willing anymore to undertake the effort. The last master puppeteer died some years ago, and the plays are rarely seen now except in amateur performances at circumcision celebrations.

Fortunately the present Turkish government, in its program of support for the preservation of the nation's Ottoman heritage, initiated in 1987 an annual Shadow Play and Traditional Turkish Theater Contest in an effort to revive this dying art. For it would be tragic to lose yet another piece of the human cultural past, not only for the Turks but for all people. In the last scene of one *Karagöz* play, the puppeteer lights a candle behind the screen and holds up his hand, saying "This is man; the burning light is the soul." Then, blowing out the candle, he says, "When the light has gone, man too disappears; only the screen, the world, remains."

Turkish Holidays and Festivals

(Note: The Turkish calendar is the same as that used in Europe and the United States, with twelve months totaling 365 days. But because Turkey is a Muslim country, it has a number of religious holidays and festivals celebrated according to the lunar calendar used throughout the Islamic world. These holidays rotate from year to year because the lunar calendar is eleven days shorter than ours, the months corresponding to phases of the moon.)

Civil Holidays

JANUARY 1 New Year's Day.

APRIL 23 Children's Day. Also National Sovereignty Day, commemorating the founding of the Grand National Assembly in Ankara in 1923. At the same time Atatürk proclaimed it as a day honoring children, the first of its kind in the world. Presently it is an international holiday by designation of the U.N.

MAY 19 Atatürk's birthday, also celebrated as National Youth and Sports Day.

AUGUST 30 Victory Day, commemorating the final victory over the Greeks in 1922 in the war of liberation.

OCTOBER 29 Republic Day, date of the proclamation of the republic by Atatürk in 1923.

NOVEMBER 10 Anniversary of Atatürk's death, marked by a moment of silence throughout the nation at precisely 9:05 A.M., the time of his death.

Religious Holidays

RECEP KANDILI First Friday in the month of Recep, the traditional date for the conception of the future Prophet Muhammad.

MIRAC KANDILI Twenty-sixth day of Recep, marking the miraculous night journey of Muhammad from Mecca to Jerusalem (Dome of the Rock) and thence to heaven.

BERAT KANDILI "Sacred night" between the fourteenth and fifteenth days of the month of Şaban; a night of watching and waiting similar to All Hallows' Eve (Hallowe'en) in Christian countries.

RAMAZAN The Holy Month or month of fasting prescribed in the Koran as one of the Pillars of Islam. During the entire month the observing Muslim lets nothing pass his or her lips during the daylight hours—no food, drink, not even licking a postage stamp. After the cannon booms to announce the end of the fast at sunset, the traditional flat *pide* bread is eaten, and then a lavish meal. It is a difficult month, particularly if Ramazan falls in the hot summer, and *Ramazan kafası* ("Ramazan head," or irritability) may cause arguments or even fights to break out. The end of Ramazan is celebrated by:

ŞEKER BAYRAMI (Also called RAMAZAN BAYRAMI), literally "Festival of Sugar." Children go door to door asking for sweets, greeting cards are exchanged, and families pay social calls on friends, relatives, and neighbors. The festival is a three-day national holiday with banks and offices closed.

KADIR GECESI The twenty-seventh day of Ramazan, the "Night of Power" when the Koran was first revealed to Muhammad and he was called to be the Messenger of God, first to his people and then the whole world. Special intercessory prayers are said on this day, and mosques illuminated.

KURBAN BAYRAMI A four-day national holiday beginning on the tenth day of the month of Zilhicce, it is the most important holiday of the year, comparable to Christmas in Christian countries. The festival commemorates Abraham's near sacrifice of his son Isaac on Mount Moriah in obedience to God; at the last moment God stayed his hand and allowed him to sacrifice a ram caught in a nearby thicket. The story is told in both the Bible (Genesis 22) and the Koran (Sura 37). Turkish families follow tradition by sacrificing a ram, if they can possibly afford to buy one; for 2.5 million sheep each year the end comes just after early prayers, when the head of the house does the slaughtering, followed by a lavish feast. Wealthy families donate much of the meat to the needy, and the skin is donated to a charity, so nothing is wasted. Kurban Bayrami is also an occasion for visiting, exchange of cards, and much traveling to visit relatives.

MEVLID-I-NEBI The anniversary of the birth of Muhammad (around A.D. 570), celebrated on the twelfth day of the month of Rebi ul-evvel with special prayers, lights and feasting.

Bibliography

Nonfiction

Addison, John, *et al. Suleyman and the Ottoman Empire.* St. Paul, MN: Greenhaven Press, 1980. For advanced students.

Akşit, Ilhan, and Ali Riza Baskan. *Ancient Civilizations of Anatolia and Historical Treasures of Turkey.* Istanbul: Güzel Sanatlar Matbaasi, 1982. An archaeological guide, with plates and photographs.

Akurgal, Ekrem. *Ancient Civilizations and Ruins of Turkey.* Istanbul: Hachette Publications, 1973. A detailed but very readable guidebook.

Bean, George. *Aegean Turkey.* New York: Norton, 1979. One of a series of archaeological guidebooks on classical sites in Turkey. Others by the same author are *Turkey Beyond the Meander* (Norton, 1980), *Turkey's Southern Shore* (Norton, 1979), and *Lycian Turkey* (Norton, 1979). Written by the "dean" of classical studies in Turkey and filled with scholarly detail, they are entertaining to read.

Benedict, Peter, *et al.,* eds. *Turkey: Geographical and Social Perspectives.* Leiden, Netherlands: Brill, 1974. A collection of useful essays on such topics as land reform, urbanization, village and regional social change, education, and so on.

Birand, M. A. *The Generals' Coup in Turkey.* London: Brassey's Defense Publishers' Group, 1987. A detailed and interesting "insider's account" of the 1980 coup, by a leading Turkish journalist.

Braude, Benjamin, and Bernard Lewis, eds. *Christians and Jews in the Ottoman Empire: The Functioning of a Plural Society.* Vol. I: *The Central Lands.* New York: Holmes & Meier, 1982. A scholarly study of the two communities in their function as *millets.*

Brosnahan, Tom. *Turkey: A Travel Survival Kit.* Berkeley, CA: Lonely Planet Publications, 1985. Part travel guide, part handbook, it is both entertaining and informative, providing valuable insights into Turkish culture and a useful historical summary.

Çelik, Zeynap. *The Remaking of Istanbul: Portrait of an Ottoman City in the Nineteenth Century.* Seattle: University of Washington Press, 1987. A fascinating work by an urban historian describing the efforts by European architects and planners to modernize the Ottoman capital, and the obstacles to modernization. Numerous photos and architects' sketches.

Davis, Fanny. *The Palace of Topkapı in Istanbul.* New York: Scribner, 1970. The best book in English on the vast imperial complex of palaces of the sultans.

Davison, Roderic H. *Turkey: A Short History.* Walkington, England: Eothen Press, 1981. For advanced students.

Goldman, Louis. *Turkey: A Week in Samil's World.* New York: Crowell-Collier Press, 1973. A Face to Face book, providing a good visual and factual introduction to Turkish life for younger readers.

Hale, William. *The Political and Economic Development of Modern Turkey.* New York: St. Martin's, 1981. A scholarly study focussing on economic development up to 1980, with a brief section on the historical evolution of the economy.

Harris, George S. *Turkey: Coping with Crisis.* Boulder, CO: Westview Press, 1985. A good basic introduction to the country.

Kağitçibaşı, Ciğdem, ed. *Sex Roles, Family and Continuity in Turkey.* Bloomington, IN: Indiana University Press, 1982. A collection of papers dealing with a number of topics important in contemporary Turkish life, such as civil violence, changing family values, and urban *gecekondu* (squatter settlements).

Karpat, Kemal. *The Gecekondu: Rural Migration and Urbanization.* Cambridge, England: Cambridge University Press, 1976. An interesting study by a research team, with extensive interviews, of three squatter settlements in Istanbul and their Black Sea village origins.

—————. *Ottoman Population, 1830–1914: Demographic and Social Characteristics.* Madison, WI: University of Wisconsin Press, 1985. An important reference work on the various communities in the empire at the time.

Kazanciğil, A., and N. Özbudun, eds. *Atatürk: Founder of a Modern State.* Hamden, CT: Archon Books, 1981. A collection of essays commemorating the 100th anniversary of Atatürk's birth.

Kinross, Lord. *Atatürk: The Rebirth of a Nation.* New York: Morrow, 1978. The best biography to date of the founder of the republic, crammed full of interesting anecdotes and illustrations.

————. *The Ottoman Centuries: The Rise and Fall of the Turkish Empire.* New York: Morrow, 1979. A readable and interesting history, though concentrated too heavily on military campaigns.

Landau, Jacob, ed. *Atatürk and the Modernization of Turkey.* Boulder, CO: Westview Press, 1984. Essays by various specialists on Atatürk's ideological, political, economic, and social ideas and how they contributed to the development of the republic.

Lewis, Bernard. *The Emergence of Modern Turkey*, 2nd ed. London: Oxford University Press, 1971. Still the standard work on the last century of empire and the rise of the modern republic.

Lewis, Raphaela. *Everyday Life in Ottoman Turkey.* New York: Putnam, 1971. A hard-to-find book that provides a good overview of life under the Shadow of God.

Muallimoğlu, Nejat. *The Wit and Wisdom of Nasreddin Hodja*, edited by Susan Knopf. New York: Cynthia Parzych Publishing Co., 1986.

Rustow, Dankwart A. *Turkey: America's Forgotten Ally.* New York: Council on Foreign Relations, 1987. A very readable book combining diplomatic history with U.S.-Turkish relations and internal political and social change.

Schick, Irvin, and Ertuğrul Tonak, eds. *Turkey in Transition.* New York: Oxford University Press, 1987. A difficult book to read but one that contains much important information on the civil violence of the '70s.

Spain, James W. *American Diplomacy in Turkey.* New York: Praeger, 1984. Primarily a memoir of the author's career in the diplomatic service, with tours as consul and then ambassador in Turkey. It includes some interesting details on the often difficult Turkish-American relationship.

Tachau, Frank. *Turkey: The Politics of Authority, Democracy and Development.* New York: Praeger, 1984. A well-written and insightful book by a long-time specialist in Turkish politics.

Walker, Barbara K., with Filiz Erol and Mine Erol. *To Set Them Free: The Early Years of Mustafa Kemal Atatürk.* Grantham, NH: Tompson and Rutter, 1981. Issued to mark the centenary of Atatürk's birth, this is a book for all ages but particularly young readers, since it deals with Atatürk's childhood and youth.

Walker, Warren S., and Ahmet E. Uysal. *Tales Alive in Turkey.* Cambridge, MA: Harvard University Press, 1966. The first lengthy collection of Turkish folktales in English, collected and translated by the authors. Of particular interest to advanced students.

Literature

Evin, Ahmet O. *Origins and Development of the Turkish Novel.* Minneapolis, MN: Bibliotheca Islamica, 1983. A study of the novel as it developed in Turkey from oral tradition to adaptation of European influences and forms.

Halman, Talat S., ed., *Modern Turkish Drama: An Anthology of Plays in Translation.* Minneapolis, MN: Bibliotheca Islamica, 1976. Translated texts of four Turkish plays from the 1960's, with an introduction by the editor, who was formerly Minister of Culture in the government and is a well-known writer and critic. The themes of the four plays range from satire on modern urban life to village-conflict issues, classical Ottoman court stories, and the retelling of classical legends (*The Ears of Midas*).

Iz, Fahir, ed. *An Anthology of Modern Turkish Short Stories.* Minneapolis, MN: Bibliotheca Islamica, 1978. A collection of short stories covering the period 1900–1975, with a brief introduction by the editor. The stories are translated by various specialists.

Filmography

The best and most complete source for films and other audio-visual resources on Turkey is *Turkey: A Precollegiate Handbook*, by Ellen-Fairbanks D. Bodman, from which this list is drawn. Ms. Bodman, Film Consultant at the University of North Carolina/Chapel Hill, has graciously reviewed this list for us.

Educational and Feature Films   The majority of the films that are available to American audiences are lent free by the Turkish Information Centers in New York and Washington. *Turkey: Emergence of a Modern Nation* (1963, 17 min., Encyclopedia Britannica) is a solid teaching film reviewing the history of Turkey from the classical period to the late 1950's.

1976 UNICEF Families of the World: Turkey (20 min., rental from University of Illinois at Champaign) is a pictorial diary of the Arslan family, who live in the village of Kabakoz some 60 miles west of Istanbul. "Study questions" are posed by the narrator and provoke thoughtful watching of the film.

The 1983 biography of Kemal Atatürk, *I Stand for Your Dreams* (60 min., 16 mm and VC, Turkish Information Center) is a careful, accurate study of this twentieth-century statesman, father of the Republic, filmed on location and drawing extensively from archival film clips and photographs. Technically excellent, and highly recommended. *Süleyman the Magnificent* (1987, 57 min., VHS, Home Vision, 5547 North Ravenswood Ave., Chicago, IL 60640–1199) was produced for the Metropolitan Museum of Art and the National Gallery of Art. Filmed on location in Turkey, this spectacular and accurate film explores the architectural and artistic achievements of the Ottoman Empire, focussing on the life and personality of Süleyman, the Lawgiver, whose sixteenth-century reign marked the zenith of Ottoman political and economic power.

Few Turkish feature films are available in the United States, although Turkey produces a large number of films each year. An exception is *Yol* (1982, 115 min.), an award-winning film by the late Yilmaz Güney. *Yol* is a panorama about five prisoners in an "open jail," each of whom represents strong political and ethnic statements. English subtitles enable American viewers to follow the story line. Women's roles, the concepts of honor, and the problems of rural communities, together with the overall strong protest against the then-current political regime and political imprisonment, all mingle in this powerful film. Such popular American films as *Topkapi* and *Midnight Express* are readily available in the United States.

Karagöz (1977, 35 min., 16 mm, rental from Indiana University at Bloomington) will introduce all to Turkish shadow theater, which has traditionally portrayed the ethnic, cultural, and social diversity of Ottoman Turkish society through characters, dialogues, costumes, music, and dance.

Additional Audio-Visual Materials

16 MM MOTION PICTURES   *Atatürk, Fifty Years Forward* (25 min., Optical Sound, produced by NATO, 1973, distributed by U.S. National Audio-Visual Center, GSA, Washington, DC 20409, available from Turkish Tourism and Information Office). This film reviews a portion of Turkey's past—largely the World War I and War of Independence periods—and demonstrates the republic's firm steps forward into the twentieth-century world of education and industrialization.

Just Say Hiç! (1969, 9 min., produced by Bailey-Film Associates; distributed by Phoenix Films). One of a number of Turkish folktales available on film, this deals with Hasan's determination to follow his master's orders despite his inability to remember what he has been told.

Ticket to Tifenni (1984, 27 min., available from the U.N. or Extension Media Center, 216 Shatuck Avenue, University of California–Berkeley, Berkeley, CA 94704, 1984) is a warm tale of a Turkish-born Minneapolis doctor who leaves his comfortable practice to return to his impoverished native village.

FILMSTRIPS   *An American Teenager Visits Turkey* (1984, 58 frames, maps, 35-minute tape cassette, produced by Barbara K. Walker and Michael Bragg under a grant from the Institute of Turkish Studies, Inc., available free, on request, from the Archive of Turkish Oral Narrative, Texas Tech University Library, Lubbock, TX 79409, or from the Turkish Tourism and Information Office in New York). The scenes here were selected by the teenager, and they prove to have appeal to audiences at all levels. The content is highly informational, ranging from a counteraction of the usual stereotypes of Turks and Turkey through foods and scenic attractions to historical background and archaeology.

Discography

Folk Music   *Folk and Traditional Music of Turkey.* New York: Folkways Records, 1961, #4404.

Village Music of Turkey. New York: Nonesuch Records, 1971. Recorded on-site in Turkey by Laxmi G. Tewari in three villages in the province of Sivas, in southeastern Turkey, these songs reflect the importance of music to members of the Alevi sect of Muslims.

For additional information regarding films and other audio-visual resources, contact the following:

Turkish Information Service
2010 Massachusetts Avenue N.W., 6th floor
Washington, DC 20036

Turkish Tourism and Information Office
821 United Nations Plaza
New York, NY 10017

Indiana University
Turkish Studies Program
143 Goodbody Hall
Bloomington, IN 47405

Landmark Films, Inc.
3450 Slade Run Drive
Falls Church, VA 22042

University of Illinois
Visual Aids Service
1325 South Oak Street
Champaign, IL 61820

The Archive of Turkish Oral Narrative
Texas Tech University Library
Lubbock, TX 79409

Index

Numbers in *italics* refer to illustrations.